Freedom
Independent
Revelation
Emancipation

Kaiserrific

FIRE is a registered trademark of Kaiserrific

Published by
Kaiserrific

ISBN-13: 978-1468125511

ISBN-10: 1468125516

Printed in the United States of America

<u>DISCLAIMER</u>

This book is strictly fictional. Everything that was written for the book was solely created for the enjoyment of the reader. All names, characters, businesses, places, events and incidents are either the products of my imagination and or used in a fictitious manner. Any resemblance to actual persons, living or dead, or actual events is purely coincidental. I wrote this book mainly from my own personal thoughts and expressions. I am apologizing now in advance for anything that I've written that is highly offensive or personal.

Dedication

My beloved grandmother, **Annie Mae Kaiser** (1928-2003) she was the matriarch of the entire Kaiser family. She taught the family how to survive and how to be our own individual by setting example from her own life. She was determined in everything that she did and passed that down onto me. A very valuable element within the keys of life that I can never take for granted. I love you always...

Michael Joseph Jackson "The King of Pop" (1958-2009) my biggest influence that surfaced my life when growing up. Never will it be a talented like him that will shine the stage as he did. Regardless as what others thought of him he has taught me and never had the chance to meet him. He said to go beyond our horizons and not to settle for limits. I have gone beyond what I thought about and here I am. God Bless You and Thank You

All the entire spoken word artists of St. Louis, Missouri that I seen hit the stage that have passed through most of the venues within the last few years in our wonderful city. I've been blessed to attend an event where I hear someone speak or spit something that they love was a truly an inspiration for me. I'd sit there and listen to each one of the performers as they touched me one way or another. With this inspiration, I gained from all of these talented people allowed me to write this book. You all have been my therapy and motivation to move forward. It was each of you all's freedom, independent, revelation, and emancipation of your lifestyles to help me create mines. Thank you and God bless you all...

Table of Contents

Chapter 4: Emancipation (Freeing Yourself from Love's Heartbreaks)

Outro: My Escape

Special Information

Acknowledgements

First and foremost I want to acknowledge and thank my heavenly father, God. Without you delivering me from the trauma, the madness, and the dramatizing experiences, I would not have been able to write this book and go forward with the rest of my life. You are the truth! Under any circumstances I cannot go a day without giving you acknowledgement.

My mother, Roslind Kaiser the one who allowed me to breathe life into the world we see in existence today. I thank God for you each and every day. If I didn't have a mother like you, I would be like a child lost in the woods. If I didn't have your mother-wit instilled in me from the time I could walk and talk, I would not be the person I am today. Again, thank you momma!

To my father, Howard Clark thanks for your support.

My beautiful son, Kemonee Kaiser you are my truest inspiration and thank you for being here. I strive for you to live out your dreams. Kid Kaiserrific I love you, Daddy

To all my family and truest friends that have been my life support since day one, you all made my dream to publish a book come alive. All of your encouragement pushed me further to continue to keep pursuing me and what I need to do with my life.

C. Lynne Luster, Kathleen Humphreys, Mea Hampton, Poet Janet Dawson and X Blu Rayne thank you all for your help on this project. You all have been truly a major asset to this book. With your help, my project has come alive to become more real to me. I look forward to more work together. We make a great team!

Big thank you to Jason Humphreys for the excellent job on the book cover! I am forever thankful for your help on this project! Your talent will be widely recognized throughout.

To all my friends in the arts (my singers, musicians, and artists) keep pushing your dreams to the extreme and I'm still waiting to see your success come the way it's well deserved.

Belle Be, Cynthia Jowers, La Vita Bell, Lyric Xpression, Kathy (Lynn) Gray, Kristy "Lightning" McKeown, Mascheria Dontell, Red October, Ronda Goolsby, and Shea Brown ten wonderful women that I've gotten to known during my journey. I thank all of you for being my support and advising me through my journey. I am forever appreciative for all of your contributions to my success. I love you all and thank you for the support.

I want to also acknowledge all the authors of poetry, short story or anything that I recently met. I appreciate all that you have contributed to my circle and continue bringing more to my surface. Your support and inspiration is highly acknowledged.

Last and absolutely the least, to all my haters... The very people who sought out to see me fail. To say that I would not become anything from my writings. The very ones who scrutinize me before they knew what I was made of and now you can see it for yourself. The very people that always had something to say but did not once see do your anything better than me. I recall one of my haters said that I will never be as talented as my other talented friends. Well, I am doing the thing and it's the first of many projects on the way.

"You are worth more than what people give you credit for." - X Blu Rayne

(*Addressed to me during a conversation in late 2010.*)

Foreword

*This young man comes to me asking for
assistance with some of his written works...
poetry, monologues and such. Now, I had never
helped anyone put a book together before. I've
edited one manuscript, was published in an
anthology and published a children's book but
never helped someone else from the ground up.
Every interaction is with purpose unbeknownst
to the people involved most often, so I accepted.
I thought maybe he hadn't begun writing at all
but once we sat down to go over what was in his
archives I quickly noticed we would need more
time than originally anticipated.*

*As he read through some of his writings, I
became engrossed with the scene, deeply
involved with the characters feelings and began
to question my own emotion. This young man
took me through the character's experience as if
I were the one feeling the love and pain. There
was anger, heartbreak, love, confusion and
elevated frustration. I saw how the characters
would move about the written work on a stage
as if in a play or one-person performance. I
saw the audience feel the extreme excitement
and unbridled rage. Deep breath. These
experiences need to be shared!*

He was given an opportunity to see his work performed LIVE and the audience was captivated with the performance to say the least. We were all on the edge of our seats waiting to see how the author embraced the character's needs and ultimately, provided for them. Believe me, not just one of his works will do this to you but the entire publication will have you wondering how the character will receive what happens next. Although I see many of these writings as stage plays, I believe I am not alone. You will see the same as you read on. You must prepare your mind to see the characters act out these pieces on your blank mental canvas.

Personally, I began to ponder how to get these writings in people's hands and hearts. I provided help with very little direction and purpose. His vision is bigger than even I can imagine. We gathered the writings just right so you, the reader, can take the journey through FIRE as the author intended. Read through the pain, listen to the men and women challenge each other to perfection and watch as the FIRE unfolds leaving you gasping for air wondering how he knows how you feel.

I am extremely thankful for the opportunity to help provide such a challenging piece of art to all who are blessed to receive it. There's something kind of brilliant about a raw, gritty, honest book that breaks you to your core as a human, makes you pick sides as a gender then

builds you up as a victor before the last page...
Something kind of brilliant. Enjoy!

~C. Lynne Luster~

Chapter 1

FREEDOM

(The Movement)

Standing Up and Speaking Out!

BE ABOUT IT

Always talking bout getting on your "A" game
Every time I hear you speak, it sounds real lame
You think you know but you just don't get it
The first to speak but always the last to get the point
Leave it to you… this happens to you every time
It's never your fault, everyone else committed the crime
You always talking about that and this
Continuing to drag yourself into a false bliss

You sit there every day on the net rhyming to other chicks' kiddy tunes
In actuality it's really giving me and everyone else the blues
BE REAL! Make sure your stuff is on point to know what you're spitting about
Spitting on issues *AND YOU DON'T EVEN KNOW WHAT THE HELL YOU TALKIN BOUT!*
Everyone's against you right and no one's ever in your corner
After you done dissin' everyone you always wonder why you end up being a loner
BE ABOUT IT!
Be about what you said you're going to do
Instead of always being the person that don't have a clue
No clue as to why things are the way they are
BE ABOUT WHAT YOU SPEAK!

FREEDOM

You keep pushing so many good people trying
to hold you up during life's struggles
But don't waste our time if you keep going in
circles

Instead of talking about it
BE ABOUT IT!
Don't blame everyone else cause you are
holding yourself back
Quit making those very distractions your usual
supply of crack
Do something to make your dreams of being a
star come alive
Instead of getting caught on certain men to
climax and satisfy your sex drive
Wasting time by listening to every one of those
dudes pitiful lies
Feeding into what they say like their
compassionate and all
But in the end, you're the only one that falls

You can sit here or there all day rhyming to all
of your flows
Not making any attempt to see where your talent
goes
I told you time and time again to pursue your
career
And as always you tell me that it's getting near
But like I thought it's always in one ear and out
the other
You remind me of a air balloon filled with lots
and lots of hot air

FIRE

And that little game that you spit to me ain't
even there

A dirty girl with good girl intentions in my mind
comes to exist
But a raw girl I'll always see you as that chick
Always falling short and remaining back on the
singles list
Keep living a false plastic life going back and
forth for sex and lust
Everything you ever dreamed and imagined
mentally will be gone like dust
But it's on you keeping the wrong company in
your life
I never said you was wrong but I know you ain't
right

I'M GOING TO BE ABOUT IT!
Show out and tell you all about it
Be something that I always wanted to become
Instead of waiting for the opportunity to come
Don't blame us! The only one person that comes
in between you and your dream is…YOU
Never allow anyone to make you the fool in
your own realities
Or your upcoming career will end up being one
in your own made up fantasies

I am going to be about my purpose in life
Almost set myself up for failure cause once I
thought you would be my wife
Giving you everything because you had the
potential to be my girl

FREEDOM

With all disappointing things you said to me
And the entire deceitful thing you did to me
And over the course of time how you made me
feel,
You left me cold at the same time lonely in this
desperate world

It's cool, so do you and I'm gonna do me
Cause I'm the same ole "C'
Once again I am still going to rise
Sing, cry, dance or laugh about it in my reprise
So when I get back to the top
I'm going to do it so well to make your mouth
drop
Achieve so good make you stop to possibly
think
Never again will I attach to you being your
weakest link
I've moved on to newer temptations and higher
heights
Not allowing anyone to block me for stepping
back into my spotlight

I am going places and seeing new things
Making my dreams filled up with happy endings
Followed up with changes for me and my entire
set
You wanna make a bet; while you're still stuck
doing the same things as always
People ain't got time your low blows and lame
blames
While you're playing continuously those same
merry-go-round games

FIRE

So for a change this time follow a piece of my
advice
I'm going to be cool and tell you as nice
I'm not gonna keep repeating the same things to
you twice
Stop talking that hot air convo
Don't keep telling yourself those lies that you
tell everyone else
Cause after awhile you going to start believe it
yourself
So be about it, make it happen
Once you do, you will see so much of a
difference
A lot of things will come to life as they come
into existence
You will have the plan that's been mapped out
for you
Be on your way with your new found groove
Shut out all the people who were no good for
you
Listen to your own thoughts instead of false
purities that's been whispered in your ear
Everything that I said to you time and time
before will become clear
But for now... ***BE ABOUT IT!***

*Dedicated to all my people who are stuck in the
game of wanting more and are too scared to try.
It's nothing to be afraid of going forward with
something you want so badly. I personally just
can't talk about it anymore. I have to be about
mines and you have to be about yours too. You
cannot continue to let people be the downfall of*

FREEDOM

*your own life. I learn from my own personal
experiences and I can tell you it's been a journey.*

-    *Kaiserrific*

EBONY ROSE
(TRIBUTE TO ALL THE
BEAUTIFUL BLACK WOMEN)

I look to you all everyday and honestly its gets
no better than that
I can't help it, you all are so beautiful
The way you all move y'all eyes, the way you
all smile, the way you all use your gestures
It's something how beautiful y'all bodies are
built
Throughout time the black woman has always
been the center of attention

Never will it be such a beautiful woman like the
black woman
So many beautiful black women have come our
way throughout the years
You have your black beauties, your gifted and
educated black women, and the realist most
down to earth black women you could ever meet
Black women will last through all of eternity
and beyond the after life

Beautiful black women who are our
grandmothers, mothers, aunts, cousins, sisters,
and friends
Embraced us on how Black America once was
and how it should always be
Black men would not have a role in society
today without the assistance of a beautiful black
woman

8

FREEDOM

I've gained my wisdom with inspiration from
two deep black women my mother and my
grandmother
Ancestry of the black woman traces back to
early civilization in Africa where she held the
crown as Queen.
A queen that was called for advice, love,
respect, and in return gained all of it
For this Black King (*me*) to cherished the Black
Queens to help rule my entire kingdom
Queens, you are still what I call of you most
beautiful black women

No need for you beautiful women to degrade
yourselves in music videos
No need for you beautiful women to walk
around anywhere with little to no clothes on
No need for you to approach a man seeking out
dirty pleasures that he can offer you
No need for you to accept the abusive treatment
these men throw out
No need to dance at no hole in the wall strip
joint showing all your precious jewels just call
yourself making a living
When you're only bringing home enough to get
a meal off the dollar menu
***STOP IT BLACK WOMEN! STOP IT! NO
NEED FOR ANY OF THIS!!!!***
No need to put out your precious body just to
get some attention or love of a man
It ain't that serious because your body is your
sacred temple so treat it with the utmost respect

FIRE

You are more than a slab of meat, more than a video vixen, more than just a few dollars and a good time

You all are a black women; an entity of your very own
The very ones who survive when times get hard
The very ones who can take care of their children and still embark a life for themselves
Make things happen because they are black women, strong women
Created by the intellect seeds of God for which you all are knowledgeable
And made from the angels in heaven to remind us what true beauty looks and sounds like

The world could not function without the contribution from the beautiful black woman
Deep women, uplifting women the very women that survive
A hurricane, an earthquake, or even a time when her utilities are disconnected
She makes sure that she has meals for her babies' everyday
Even if there's no food in the house and all she has is canned goods
Black women have experienced the meaning of struggle and shown us the examples of survival

A woman that gets less acknowledgment or no recognition in this country is the black woman
In the past, black women were viewed as your whores, maids, servants

FREEDOM

And not as a queens or public figures
Look at the old films in black and white and you
will see how degrading black women were
viewed compared to white America in the
1920's, 30's, 40's and 50's
They represent your legacy in such shame
Had it not been for women like Harriet T,
Sojourner T, Coretta K, and Michelle O
There would be no fight for change and peace
among the races
Not been for writers like Zora H, Alice W,
Terry M, and Toni M
Who fought to paved the way for black female
writers in African American literature
It would not be writers out here writing things
that expresses who the black woman is as an
individual
Had it not been for Phyllis W, Maya A, Nikki
G, and Gwendolyn B
Who gave their prospective on literature from a
black woman's point of view?
Would not be inspiring strong female poets now
writing to be more liberated and expressive

Thank you beautiful black women
Thank you for the contribution to our beautiful
race
Thank you for loving your husbands and
supporting them no matter what
Making them feel like somebody again with
motivation
Motivating our black men to be men and to
work hard for their families

FIRE

Thank you for being a mother and raising these
children to become responsible adults
Thank you for waking up each morning to make
sure the babies are off to school
For sitting up each and every night helping them
with their homework
Pushing the education into their brains so
inspire them to be anything they set out to do
that productive
Keeping the kids in line when they're about to
get into trouble
Thank you mommas for loving us
unconditionally throughout all of our success
Thank you grandmommas for providing wisdom
with love

Beautiful black women all over the
world...*THANK YOU!!*

FREEDOM

"EMANCIPATION/RECLAIM!"

Today I am free from everything that has ever
bothered me
Emancipated from the evils of man to the
destruction of the mind
I removed all negativity and claimed a new
positive life as mine

I am more than what people expect for me to be
I am a role model that many will follow
I will not submit to life made by others
I refuse to be the slave of others
I am a king and a king is how I shall live

I LIVE FOR ME!
AND DO MY THING!
I WILL NOT BE MADE A FOOL AND MIND
WILL FOREVER BE A TREASURE ONLY I
CAN KEEP!

For some years now I have not been the person I
once was. With that I had become closed in a
shell becoming very unhappy. I looked in the
mirror one morning to see a person that I was
not pleased with. I said to myself it's time to do
something about it. Something just came over
me to reclaim my life for the best. I been trying
to remove this stains in my life and I said damn
it's time to let go and re-invent who I am. I am
ready to reclaim who I am and I thank everyone
for your support but I must walk this journey
alone. I'm about to go through challenges in my

FIRE

life. It will be people that will not agree with who I am becoming or what I am doing. But I can't make their feelings and concerns be my focus. My focus is me and that's all that matters. Please stand by with what I am saying and you see a new and improved KAISERRIFIC!

I am still a writer. I have a line of books that will be coming my way. Whether its poetry, fiction, plays, or storytelling you will know that I wrote it. I will not be stopping at just one project I have so much more to look forward to and you will be satisfied with it.

I am an educator. I will continue to teach or inform anyone information that they would like to know. You are never too old to learn. In the times we live in, much knowledge is needed in order to survive the reality of this world.

I am still a singer and dancer. I will continue to perform and even get some more training. Music and singing has always been my first love even before writing. I think back to all the great singers and dancers that influenced me in my younger days to chase my dreams and to become something that I always wanted. Best believe it will be better than how it was when I first started.

I am still an actor. I will go out and audition for any part that I can get my hands on. I will continue to write scripts, film, and direct. I plan

14

FREEDOM

to make a return to world that I was introduced
when I was 15 years old. Become as good as
anyone I seen or heard of in Hollywood or on
Broadway. I am a star and a celebrity by my
own right!

I am still a father. I will continue to love my
son and cherish his thoughts and ideas. I have to
be a model so that he can follow and become
something greater than I ever will be. I just
don't want him to suffer or struggle as I have
before in my life. So I continue out to make the
best for him.

I am still a man. I have a job to do and I will
not allow anyone to block me from my glory. If
one man can stand up to the downfall, other men
can stand up to face the issues of the world.
Continue to be strong and move forward.

I am still a friend. I will be there for you all but
I can't live in your dreams. I have to live in mine
and make it special and stand out from anything
I have done. I have faith in every one of you
and you all have made me so proud. Don't
worry I will be there for your functions and
moments that will have your eyes blowing up.

I am emancipated and now it's time for me to
venture to the world.
Take on everything that has been blocking me
all these years.
Stomp on my fears for I am in control

FIRE

Crush the happiness of the devil and his
supporters who don't think that I can make it
And broke the grip of failure that held me for so
long
The very ones that wanted me to fail instead of
succeeding...

I AM EMANCIPATED....

"Free at last,
Free at last.
Thank God Almighty,
I'm free at last..."

       - Dr. Martin Luther King Jr.

FREEDOM

POLITICS

MAN, FUCK POLITICS!
What the fuck kind of difference is it going to
make when I don't see any of our people
making a difference?
Get your ass out the house and vote!
This country is not ran just by the President or
the people that do vote
It's ran by yo ass too; so your vote matters
But believe me the whole political campaigns
ain't shit either

I don't see why we vote and then the appointed
person we didn't want gets elected
It's just another experiment to see how dumb we
can be
And y'all asses are proving it to the system each
and everyday
See I vote and make it my business to get to the
polls
Make it my purpose to get the politicians that
are for me than against me at least

Yeah we have a black President but what can he
do if you don't get your ass up and vote
Then you want to cry to the government about
no funding for education
Or no support in getting jobs for the
unemployed
And I get tired of those women that are
consistently abusing the welfare assistance

17

FIRE

Some political beliefs ain't shit without the use
of our minds and our votes

You know we cannot afford the gas at the
stations because of oil issues with other
countries,
As the President encourages congress to
approve the energy bill
But some people can't get their ass up and go
vote so the damn gas prices go down
It can benefit you by having your utilities prices
go down and save yo ass some money
The money you put into paying all those bills
can be money to go to a savings account
Or to purchase a proper meal at the grocery
store for you and your loved ones
Or maybe it can be money saved keeping the
world from being so money hungry

But let's get on the politicians for a minute
They want to run these big state of the art
campaigns and don't promise what they gone do
once in office
Remember a promise is to be kept and not
broken but shit they break laws for all that
matters
People are so quick to jump on the President for
shit that the last President allowed in his term
Wake up! These politicians say things only to
get your vote
These elections are so full of shit; they want our
money more than our vote

FREEDOM

See and that way they don't have to pull out of
pockct
Do the homework; don't wait for anyone to
come do it for you
Know what you punching them holes in for at
the voting poll

Now when everyone is not satisfied with who
was elected into office,
Those selected persons that didn't go vote are so
quick to point the finger at the next person
We are at blame because we did not go hard
enough
And encourage our friends, family, or love ones
to make a difference
We didn't tell them why it's important that they
vote
We didn't remind them how it was someone's
mother, father, sister or brother that got lynched
for going to vote
Tied to a tree burned to ashes, all because he or
she wanted to get their vote reached in these
country political views
Or how our great-great-great-grandparents had
to take a literacy test just to vote,
And if they didn't pass the test they could not
vote!

Are you telling me that my descendents were
too dumb to elect a person they wanted in
office?
Did our vote not matter? *TELL THE TRUTH
DAMN IT!!!*

FIRE

You saying that when people sat in for protest
and marched for civil rights
We don't have a right to go into the little booth
and cast our votes
That was their way of screwing us over

Just like the presidential election of 2000
All ballots were not counted and some were lost
The same way they screwed us like 130 years
before
Then to elect a man into office that did not do
anything when this country was under attack by
terrorists
**IF YOU LOOK AT THE DAMN VIDEO, HIS
DUMB ASS WAS CLUELESS AS I DON'T
KNOW WHAT!!!**
Is that what you all want back in
office…another fuck up!

What do we need to do to get you out there to
vote?
A free box of chicken and some Kool-Aid to go
with that for your vote?
I hate to sound racist and stereotypical about it,
BUT DAMN!
What can we do, brothers and sisters, to get
your vote to matter?
Brothers, you get your point across when you're
trying to sleep with a woman
Or sisters it's not hard getting money from a
man that will give it to you for that club outfit
**SO IT'S NOT HARD TO GET OFF YO ASS
TO GO VOTE!**

FREEDOM

Just make that one stop to the voting polls on
Election Day,
And vote the right people into office!

I got my vote casted and I am voting for winners
Electing people who are going to make a
difference for this unbalanced country
Make a change for the better
Let's stop bringing fuck ups into our Senate,
House of Representatives, or even into the
White House.

MAKE A DIFFERENCE AND VOTE!

FIRE

RAGED BLACK MAN

I AM SO MAD!
You have no idea what kind of country we live in
Anything goes in their eyes 'cause they make the laws
But am I suppose to be the good citizen and support all the politicians?
WELL FUCK YOU CROOKED POLITICIANS AND YOUR BELIEFS!
I got my own beliefs that I am going by

For one I am a *MAN!*
I AM A BLACK MAN, DAMN IT!
You better respect me and I will respect you!
You can respect me by using my proper name
My name is not nigger, negro, darky, or any of that
Call me the name that my momma named me at the hospital!

When I make my entrance, I expect to walk through the front door of the hotel
And not through the kitchen like you did other black celebrities
Can't tell me that I can't dine in this restaurant cause of my skin color
FUCK YOU, NOW TAKE MY ORDER AND GIVE ME THE BEST STEAK OF MY CHOICE!
IF YOU DON'T I WILL BE RAISING ALL KINDS OF HELL UP IN HERE!

FREEDOM

See my people have already suffered over 400
years of torture in this country
AND YOU THINK ONE MINUTE I'M
GONNA LET YOU TREAT ME LIKE SHIT!
YOU BETTER WATCH WHAT YOU SAY TO
ME BEFORE I PUT THIS KNIFE
THROUGH YOUR THROAT!
See I try to come to you civilized and calm but
you make me rational to being outraged
But its people like you that make me sick,
thinking you can walk and talk to me any kind
of way…
But what pisses me off is the people that are not
saying anything!

You know like the people that didn't say
anything when Emmett got killed
By two white men all because one wife said that
he flirted with her by whistling
Bitch, if I came in the store and whistled at
you….what the fuck you gon do?
I would be posted up all night waiting on your
husband and his friend
I GOT A SOME BULLETS TO GO RIGHT IN
THEIR ASSESS!!!
NOT GON COME TO ME DISRESPECTING
ME AND HAVE THE DAMN NERVE TO
TRY AND KIDNAP ME TO KILL ME!
FUCK YOU DUDE AND YOUR PUNK
PUSSY ASS FRIEND!
GOT THE NERVE TO GET OFF AT THE
TRIAL!

FIRE

What about the freedom riders that were killed
by the police back in '64?
I WOULDN'T ALLOW A COP TO PLACE
THEIR RACIST HANDS ON ME!
WE WOULD HAVE BEEN READY FOR A
FIGHT!
THREE COPS WOULD HAVE BEEN
MISSING!
I WOULD HAVE HAD NO MERCY FOR
THEIR RACIST SOULS!

But what gets under my skin is black folks that
are quiet trying to protect their lives
If you stand up and set these crackers straight,
then it would be no race issues...
ITS MORE OF US THAN OF THEM!
TAKE THEIR SHIT AND MAKE THEM CRY
LIKE LITTLE BITCHES!
SEE THEY WERE NOT GOING TO SIT
THERE AND LIE TO ME!
TELL ME THAT I'M GETTING FORTY
ACRES AND A MULE!
I'D RATHER BE HOMELESS GOING
FROM CITY TO CITY
THEN TO TELL ME THAT I CANNOT
LEAVE THE SLAVE COUNTY UNTIL I
PAID OFF AN UNKNOWN DEBT
HOW THE FUCK DO I HAVE DEBT WHEN
SLAVES BEEN WORKING FOR Y'ALL
ASSES ALL THOSE YEARS?!!!!!

24

FREEDOM

SO YOU STUPID ASS PEOPLE WE DIDN'T
HAVE ANYTHING TO LEAVE A DEBT
WITH
WE WERE FREE AND THAT'S WHAT
HAPPENED!

If I was around I would have educated our black
people that we didn't owe them anything and we
were able to leave at any given time.
I am not shamed of my people; they did what
they had to do in order survive
Mothers protect their children
Fathers work hard in the fields
While we have an over seer watching our every
move…
You can watch these nuts! You fucking pigs!!!!

But you know I am not going to fault all white
people
You actually have good white people that
actually care about all of us
'Cause God blessed them from birth to be that
way
I thank you for being kind to us and being one
with us
BUT ITS THOSE IGNORNANT
MOTHERFUCKERS THAT PISSES ME
OFF!
LIKE THEM BITCH ASS MEN IN THE
WHITE SHEETS!!!!

FIRE

ANYTIME YO BITCH ASS HAVE TO HIDE
YOUR IDENTITY THROUGH BED
SHEETS!
REALLY TELLS ME HOW MUCH BITCH
YOU GOT IN YOU!!!
HOW WOULD YOU LIKE IT IF I GOT
SOME BLACK SHEETS?
COME AT YOU WITH, INSTEAD OF A
CROSS WITH FIRE IN YOUR YARD,
I PUT A PEACE SIGN LIT UP IN FLAMES
AND HANG YOU FROM A TREE YOU
WHITE DEVILS WOULD NOT BE HAPPY!
WOULD THEY LIKE IT IF WE
HUMILIATE THEM NATIONALLY ON TV
FILM
IN PUBLIC SUCH AS A PARADE
SAYING BLACK POWER
SAYING LETS KILL THEM WHITE
DEVILS!
THEY WOULD CALL IN THE NATIONAL
GUARD OR ANY FORCE THAT WILL
PROTECT THEM!
BUT THAT'S CRAZY!
SHOW YOUR FACE!!!!
BE THE PERSON! YOU TALK SO MUCH
SHIT BEHIND THEM WHITE SHEETS!

TAKE YOUR LITTLE BITCH ASSES BACK
HOME!
AND PUT YOUR SHEETS BACK IN THE
CLOSET BEFORE THE WIFE GETS MAD!
YOUR BITCH ASSES PROBABLY LIVING
WITH Y'ALL MOMMAS

FREEDOM

WOULD I BE WRONG TO BUILD A LARGE
ENOUGH SHIP
AND CAPTURE ALL THE RACISTS
PRICKS TO PUT THEM IN CHAINS
WHOOP THEIR ASSES WITH A WHIP!
PHOTOGRAPH ALL THEIR WHIP
MARKS!!!

BUT BELIEVE IT OR NOT WE LIVE IN
MODERN SLAVERY!
Slaving at a job 40 hours a week to get a
paycheck
Not moving forward still stuck in the same place
from when you started
We refer to the job as a plantation, gone at the
end of the day and back the next day bright and
early
And with promising benefits that we don't seem
to get 'cause they are so quick to fire us

I AM A MAN!
I AM A RAGED BLACK MAN!
I CAN'T LIVE WITH THIS MADNESS!!!

SOCIETY

You're known for judging other people that are
not like you
You're a master at bringing someone down
instead of bringing them up
You have killed a lot of good people and ruined
the careers of some
You have become skilled at making some
insecure about their self esteem

Society, I hate you
I hate you for exactly who you are
***AN IGNORANT, MISUNDERSTOOD,
SELFISH SON OF A BITCH!!!***
I hate you for hurting people like me with
wonderful personalities
You're wrong for making asses out of anyone
that did not fit inside of your circle
How dare you say in order to fit in we need
dress and act a certain style?

Society, you existed so far back when people
were young and their peers were always teasing
With no idea as to how they were going to be
treated
I was so wrong for wanting to belong to a class
of people with no purpose in life
I never want to fit into a circle with a bunch of
lames like you society
I am so superior and don't have to prove
anything to you or to anybody

FREEDOM

Your technique is simple that it easily destroys
lives in the matter of minutes

You get inside the people's minds to inform
them that because they are not wearing the
newest clothes,
The newest tennis shoes from the store that cost
way over $100.00,
Leading to hanging out with the coolest people
in the industry of school, music, and tv
Listening to the music that is on everyone's
radio, CD player, or mp3 player
You call them all sorts of names like losers
putting them beneath you
But I don't see what you're doing to help this
person get the best
I don't see you helping these people get on their
feet
You're selfish with your own wants and needs
just like the next person
You ain't any better than a dirty old politician in
a campaign trying to win my vote

SOCIETY I'M TIRED OF YOU TREATING
ME LIKE SHIT!!!
I REFUSE TO TAKE YOUR ABUSE
ANYMORE!!!
You're not going to make me feel like a statistic
in the everyday world
And to think that I wanted to fit in with these
egotistical inhabitants
I am so damn mad at myself for thinking I can
fit in with a group of people,

FIRE

That have nothing in common with me; sad to
say never will
Stop trying to corrupt my mind to put down
another man or another woman for being less
fortunate as I once was

ALL THE SUPPORTERS OF SOCIETY CAN
KISS MY ASS!!!
KICK ROCKS!!!
I'M GOOD ON YOU PEOPLE TOO!!!
I REFUSE TO ALLOW MY MIND TO BE
SET UP, CORRUPTED BY YOUR ACTIONS
AND WORDS!
I DON'T NEED THAT BULLSHIT!
I REFUSE TO GIVE INTO YOU, THE
ENEMY
I am so outraged out at Society
Takes the intelligent minds of people like you
and hurt people like me
I wanted to be apart of a Society that once was
so cool to me at the time
But I come to learn that they're some real
assholes

Put me down because I act a certain way
Sing or dance to certain dances that you don't
do
Dress in certain kind of clothes that are not of
your fashion etiquette
Smile or talk a certain way that will classify
who I am
WHO THE FUCK ARE YOU TO CLASSIFY
ME!

FREEDOM

The very ones I'm talking about go behind my
back to question my sexuality,
To have the fucking nerve to place me in a
category that is not me!
*I DON'T GIVE YOU THE PRIVILEGE FOR
MY NAME TO COME OUT YOUR MOUTH!*

So if I changed the style of my hair to please
you
(I CHANGE MY HAIR FOR NOBODY!!)
Make my voice sound more like a person you'd
be interested in talking to
*(I LOVE MY VOICE AND THAT'S TOO
BAD!!)*
Sing the songs that are continuously on the
radio, would that get your bodies moving?
*(DON'T KNOCK MY SONGS BECAUSE I
DON'T DISPLAY THAT KIND OF TALENT
LIKE YOU!!)*
Dress in certain clothes of your requirements for
you to be around me
*(YOU DON'T BUY MY CLOTHES, SO YOU
HAVE NO SAY SO ON MY DRESS
ATTIRE!!)*
Or share the same views as any other ingrate in
this "Society"
Then would allow you to be in your circle?
*I'M BETTER OFF WITHOUT YOU!!!
FUCK OFF SOCIETY, YOU SOCIAL
DISEASE!
BEFORE I GET THE SAME SYMPTOMS
THAT WOULD MAKE ME AS IGNORANT
AS YOU!*

FIRE

Excuse me but Society needed to know how I
felt about them
Society comes into your life pretending to be
your friend
While you're at your peek of being successful
and on top making it big
Society pulls out the champagne celebrating
your victory as if it was theirs
But the minute you fall on your back,
Be so quick to spread your name all in the dirt
Like your spiteful ex-girlfriend or boyfriend
seeking vengeance

Society has ruined some of the most known
celebrities and public figures even from the
grave
Like Michael who is dead now because Society
put him through so much stress
At the peak of his career and fame, you, Society
loved and cherished him
A gifted singer, extraordinary entertainer who
worked hard all of his life to spread love and
peace among everyone
Once the media attacked him, you turned your
back
Allowing everyone to say terrible things about
him
Put his name all in mud making him look and
feel like an outsider
Now he is gone, you and your supporters come
out like roaches

FREEDOM

Out of nowhere pretending to mourn his loss
and missing him
When you all were the same people that lead
him to his grave
HE WAS TOO YOUNG TO DIE!!!
NEVER GOT TO LIVE AN OLD LIFE!!!
The record label profiting money off his God-
given talent now that he is no longer with us
Where were you in his defense when he needed
us the most?
I know he felt that we all turned our backs on
him

Or what about Malcolm and Martin, both good
men that stood for something they both believed
in
Fought to defend black people that were judged
by you, Society, because of their skin color
Making it hard for black people to live out a
normal life in a country full of racism and
hatred
These two educated young gentlemen were both
world leaders by right until they were snitched
on by Society
Only because you, Society, felt they had too
much power
And died by the result of a bullet, a bullet that
you, Society, marked their names on in cold
blood

Speaking out on racism, Society do you
remember the little boy Emmett?

33

FIRE

Do you remember how you allowed him to be dragged out of his family home in the middle of the night?

To be beaten up, kicked, and mutilated all because he was lied on

Saying that he was flirting by whistling to that white woman in the store

Because you didn't stand up and defend this boy, his body had to be carried out of the Tallahatchie River

They mutilated his body so bad he couldn't be identified as a 14 year old boy

Why didn't you save this boy's life from being hit with that cotton gin fan to that barbed wire being tied around his neck?

Where were you society when this mother cried out about what you didn't do to help her son?

THIS WOMAN CRIED OUT!!! HER SON CRIED OUT FOR HIS LIFE!!!

AND YOU DID NOTHING! NOTHING!

How did you feel when she displayed her child's body for America to see what you allowed happen?

Why, Society, did you allow this woman to live out the rest of her life carrying the guilt for her son's death?

This could have been one of your children and if you saved him, he would be alive today

BUT AS CLEAR AS I SEE IT, SOCIETY THINK ABOUT SOCIETY AND NO ONE ELSE!

FREEDOM

So Society, where were you on September 15,
1963
When four little girls were killed the basement
of their church
Society, did your heart reach out to the families
of these girls
Did you tell who did it and why they did it?
No, you remain in the shadows as always
Did you give any justice for the families that
loss these innocent little girls?
Babies who have become someone very
important in our community?
*NO! AS ALWAYS YOU THOUGHT ABOUT
YOU!!!*
AND SAVED YOUR OWN LIFE!!!
*YOU ALLOWED THOSE MEN TO GET
AWAY!!!*
*OH BUT SOCIETY, YOU KNOW YOU FELT
THE GUILT PLACED UPON YOU FOR
KILLING A CHILD!!!*

This world we live with Society nobody is
safe…so protect you!!!

WHAT NOW! WHAT NOW!
Society, are you trying to crucify me like you
did Jesus Christ?
You're not trying to befriend me in my face
To learn my teachings; ask for my help to heal
you from your tribulations
Then have your Society try me for not being one
of you

FIRE

I REFUSE TO LET YOU HANG ME ON A
CROSS AND TAKE MY LIFE!!!
Well you can't destroy me; I am too immortal
for your nonsense

Remember people, we are still being crucified in
our minds today by Society
Listening to that bullshit that your Society has to
offer
It's displayed in our media
TV shows are filled with Society's despiteful
lies and trickery
THEN EVERYONE WANTS TO JUMP AND
JOIN THE BANDWAGON!!!
The news reports only the bad stories in the
black communities
But never the good of what someone has done
in the community
Like the non-profit organizations that help
children, the elderly or the homeless
WHAT ABOUT THOSE PEOPLE? THEY
DESERVE RECOGNITION!!!
Radio displays some of Society's finest
The music our young generations listen to

Society is a backstabber
So be careful who you keep as your company
Remember the people that are in your corner
SOCIETY YOU BASTARD, YOU WONT GET
THE BEST OF ME!!!
I am freed from your judgment and opinions
I've gained my independence from you and will
never be regretted

FREEDOM

Friends, let us make a toast,
*A TOAST TO MY INDEPENDENCE FROM
SOCIETY AND THEIR FUCKED UP
ISSUES!
NO MORE DISCRIMINATION BY WHO WE
ARE!!!
NOW SOCIETY GO SCRUTINIZE ME ON
THAT!*

STORM OF BLACK

Wake up brothas and sistas!!!
I am clearly bringing something to your
attention
Black people are in need of major change
We all need to go under serious construction
And this really needs to be fixed immediately

I see too many things going on with our people
Everyone's priorities are more of their options
We are not paying attention to the fact that we
are the most disliked race on the planet
They know who I am talking about
Look down at us and observe every little thing
that we do
And you are too blind to even notice that
But you keep roaming around here not doing
anything

Yeah tell me to do something about it since I am
concerned
But one man can't change everything
It takes us a whole, a whole race, a whole nation
But it starts with self first!
But how can you do that if you don't love your
own race

We've already proven that we are skilled in
entertainment and sports
We let them know that we have skills in hair,
food, and other trades

FREEDOM

We can become anything that we want to be!
Lawyers – we can defend our people because you already know that the court wants us in a cage
Teachers – we can teach ourselves to move forward because "you know who" wants us to not have knowledge because they fear us taking over this land….But HA! That's too late it's in the making!
Doctors – we can cure each other instead of allowing "you know who" continue giving us medicines when really it's another disease to keep bringing us back to their business and make more money off of us.
Fire Fighters - we can show that we can save a life just as much as how the media say how we take a life.
Bankers and Business Owners – We can make our own money legally! We don't need to work our asses off for another person to move a company up! Make your business what it is so that there is no dependency. Bring back the businesses in the black community.
LET THEM KNOW THAT BLACK PEOPLE ARE MORE THAN JUST A PUPPET ON STRINGS!!!!
Anything we want to be that will be a positive influence on our people
A great impact on the community!
THIS BEEF AND CONTINUOUS FIGHT WITH EACH OTHER HAS TO STOP!!
We need to end this hatred with each other
We are a storm of black

FIRE

WE COVER THE ENTIRE LAND!!!
WE WERE PLACED HERE FOR A
REASON!!
AND AS A STORM WE COVER TOGETHER
AS UNIT, A WHOLE!!!
I love black
I love the race that defines us
Black is beautiful and beautiful is black
Our people are beautiful
Our men are strong, gifted
Our women are loving and real
We got talent and know how to use it so well
Some of the most intelligent people I know are
black

But let me talk about what's going on with our
black race
The race that needs more unity than all the other
races that ever existed
When will we stop hating each other because we
are different?
When can we sit down and talk in a civilized
manner without guns?
Why must we always diss each other which it
leads to someone killing another?

From what other races say,
We are ignorant
We are lazy
We are dumb and can't finish school
We don't want more out of life
We are a disgrace to the country

FREEDOM

And sad to say it comes from some of our own
people!

What happened to our business?
We turn to other people and help them make the
money
When we do get a business, the service is so bad
Make you not want to deal with a bad business
And the other people can always win us over
You better be careful or might be too late
The business might be taken from up under you

As we are losing our businesses!!!
Black people, we are losing our respect!!!
Our dignity has been long gone taken from us!!!
WE NEED TO STOP THIS!!!
THEY ARE GETTING THE BEST OF US!!!!

Black men, what's up?
What are you doing as men to provide for your
children?
How are you taking care of home?
I know standing on the street hustling selling
weed is not doing it
Why not go out and find a job?
Wait a minute; don't tell me all the jobs are
taken
Start your own business (besides going out
selling drugs)
Find a skill that will make you some money!
Let the others know that men are more than just
baby makers
Drug dealers and addicts

FIRE

Haters of their own people because they are
doing well
Lazy bums
We are more than thieves and men that sit
around playing the game all day
*INFORM THEM THAT WE ARE NOT
EACH OTHER'S ENEMIES!!!!*
We are more than the men they say disrespect
our women
Show them that you love your black
women...*LET IT BE SEEN!!!*
Let them know you are not a *NIGGER!!!*
*LET THEM KNOW YOU ARE A BLACK
MAN!!!*
A PROUD MAN!!!
STRONG MAN!!!
*READY TO TAKE THAT SOCIETY
DOWN!!!*
*LET THEM KNOW THAT YOU ARE MORE
THAN WHAT YOU ARE MADE OF!!!*

Black woman, what's up?
You got other races thinking you all are hoes!
The way you dress
Walking around with colors of the rainbow in
your head
With hair that came off the ass of a horse
You are being observed by the way you speak to
people
They and I mean they (*you know who I am
talking about*)
Feel like you all are lazy

FREEDOM

Use a man to get knocked up so that you can have a check coming in
Waiting on welfare checks and child support to take care of your needs
Make them look like liars because you are nothing like that!

You can't let our black men sit around and call you a bitch
But it's ok for you ladies to call each other bitches
Then you walk around with all these artificial objects while your children are looking a mess
Come on sistas!
Let it be known that you all are not how we characterized on TV
MAKE THEM TAKE BACK WHAT THE MEDIA HAS PORTRAYED YOU!!!
Reality shows, making you all sound like you all have nothing better to do with yourself
All in music videos being the main hoe on the screen
SHAKING YO ASS EVERY CHANCE YOU GET THINKING ITS CUTE!!
Make them look like liars!
Make them feel stupid!
Tell them you are a *BLACK WOMAN!*
A PROUD WOMAN!!!
A STRONG WOMAN!!!
AND YOU REFUSE TO ACCEPT THEIR SLAVE MENTALITY BULLSHIT!!!

FIRE

*WATCH OUT! A STORM OF BLACK IS
COMING YOUR WAY!!!*

TO BE CONTINUED...

FREEDOM

TRUTH

We sometimes speak of the truth
Some know the truth as told to them
Others listen to the truth from anyone who
speaks it
But to you, what is the truth?
No one can really know that

See I am just like you or the next person
I have flesh and bones made of nerves and cells
I have the hunger for success just like most
people will do anything to get it
I want more in my future and I expect more to
come out of it

Again, what is truth?
How do you get the truth?
Do we ask?
Do we cry out for it?
Do we ever sell our souls to the devil for it?
Maybe one day the truth will be revealed

One day our young children will be adults
Maybe they will have the truth for us
Provide the answers to my Y
Maybe they have a story to tell with their truth
and experience
Only time will tell what truth will be spoken on

But for now teach our babies
Love our babies
Understand our babies

FIRE

And in return they will give it back to you

Now that is the truth...

FREEDOM

WHO WE ARE....MEN!

I KNOW WHO I AM!
Don't call me a boy!
You don't have to remind me,
I AM A MAN!
I have feelings just like women
You don't have to tell me twice about what I
need to do
I know how I need to go make things right
It's so hard for us men at times
Women don't understand that we go through
things too
We go through a struggle here and there too!

Please don't mistake me for an asshole
Women, when are you all going to stop labeling
us as deadbeats?
I know what I am suppose to do for my children
You all have a tendency to think that we won't
raise ours
But yet you think we go out to raise another
woman's babies

We do not intentionally try to abandon ours to
raise theirs
We meet a woman to love and care just like you
do when you meet a new man
But really you're just mad because we do not
love you anymore
When we wanted to love you, you turn your
back on us
So we decided to find love elsewhere

FIRE

That's just the way things are maybe one day
you'll learn

But I am a strong minded man with a lot to offer
Some of these other men make me look bad
They leave a bad taste in a lady's mouth when
the new man enters
Next thing I hear from some women that all
men are the same
Maybe if you ladies didn't compare us then
maybe you wouldn't get the same treatment
You only get what you deserve cause of how
you treat the men

Some men don't know day from night
Sitting around in the house playing the game
When they could be out providing and making a
way for their families
Yes, I try to provide for my family with what I
got till I get more
Yet this is what some women allow
But I don't need a woman that's ok with me not
doing anything with myself
And yet some of us men take and bank on it
I need a woman that will stay on me about my
priorities versus my options
Ladies what does that tell us about you?

See a man will only do what a woman allows
him to do
But you ladies are so quick to say that he got it
from his momma

FREEDOM

Don't blame momma because you are allowing
the same thing to happen
Then you run downtown to the support agencies
to garnish money out of this man check
Remember it takes two to make a baby...
We know that it's a man's responsibility to raise
a child
But how can we when you don't give us the
credit to be a man
We look for jobs too
But the unemployment rate is so high
I thought it would be easy to find a job with
some men not wanting to work
But when do we get a break?
**DAMN! PLEASE SHOW US SOME KIND
OF RESPECT!!!**

Ladies, some of you ask too much from us men
You want to know if we got a bank account and
if we do how much we got in it
Listening to the ads on the chatline and I hear
what you all are requesting
Saying that you are looking for a man with his
own house, car, and an established job
I say damn, what the hell you have to match us?
Then when we meet that lady, she ain't living
no better than me

Some men don't ask for a whole lot in a woman
But the ones that are able to handle a woman in
their league
But to date a woman nowadays, it equal outs to
applying for a job

FIRE

Only difference, I am not sending a resume or
getting set up for an interview
So when the supply and demand went up so did
women's standards
What happened to people coming together to
grow on each other

Some women accept a man that has nothing but
refuse the ones that's trying to make something
Bringing any man into their homes
Not caring if they are any good for your
children
And he be the one doing everything under the
sun to you
If he was to steal from you, he could
If he was to cheat on you, he should
If he was to break your heart, he would
And as always you take him back

Some men take that bullshit and run with it
Why buy the cow; when you can milk them for
free?
Before you know it they are stealing the milk
But that's just how your loving men operates
But fellas we ain't fully innocent in all of this

Don't sit here and think we are always the
victim
We add flame to the fire too
If we learn to treat our women with respect
maybe we can keep a decent woman
A woman wants attention, to be noticed, and
complimented

FREEDOM

**NOT ALWAYS BE TREATED LIKE
SHIT!!!**
But when you're a boy trying to fill a man's
shoes that's what you get
A BOY!!!
And thinking like that, that is all you will ever
be…
Women need a strong man that can stand on his
own
A man that will go to any extreme to provide for
him, her, and the family
Women look for us men to have some
establishment
Being a drug dealer or part time hustler doesn't
qualify
Saying your upcoming rapper with no demo or
single out doesn't qualify
GET YOUR SHIT TOGETHER!!!

Finish or return to school take up a trade or find
a job
Better yet find you a career that will set you off
for life
Apply yourself to something instead of waiting
on some to apply it for you
Let go of the old tired game
This ain't how to be a playa
Show some responsibility and you will see
where credit is given

Women are more than your in-house slave
Your personal cook
More than just in-house pussy

FIRE

She is your friend
Your backbone through the good and the bad
You are her support system too

Don't allow anyone to degrade who you are
Keep your head up continue forward
Go forward and don't look back!
We got a task to complete because this is who
we are...
Men and that's our mission

We are men and men are what we are. I see so many young men go downhill to become old men with nothing to show. They are wandering around with nowhere to go, nowhere to live or sleep. So easily criticized for not having this or not having that. This becomes one of the biggest excuses that women say why they don't want to give us a chance. Man walking around seeking for love in all the wrong faces being in the wrong places. Men desperately being gone in the middle of the night sexing any woman because of the lack of love instead of searching for a soul mate. Then you have men that plant seeds all over the places but don't want to be responsible for their children. Then it becomes an argument between man and woman. Next thing you know she is waiting on money taken from your check put on her card. Then it's a tension because the two of you still love each other but with other people. When the man show his new

FREEDOM

woman attention that he once showed you; the other woman be so quick to blame the other for mistreating the children. Men stand up and take responsibility and become the better person. Work on an agreement that you can work out to make things right. We are men and we are superior so STEP UP!

- *Kaiserrific*

Chapter 2

INDEPENDENT

(Standing Up for Self)

Don't Be Afraid to Define Who You Are!

INDEPENDENT

DEFINE ME

WHO DEFINES ME?
I define me…
I define what I represent
I ask that you respect me as I am
But yet… I don't get that treatment
With you negative definitions of me under your
scandalous tone…
You call me your friend
You try to define me with your pessimistic
visions of my success… Negotiating the level of
strength that lies within my determination.
Oh I hear you… is he an artist? Does he have
what it takes? He hasn't done anything since his
younger years…
Humph… I know I haven't done anything in a
long time ***BUT WHO ASKED YOU?!***
 I am still an artist and ***MY SUCCESS WILL
NOT BE DEFINED BY THE LIKES OF YOU***
So understand who defines me… *I DEFINE
ME*

WHAT DEFINES ME?
My personality
My character
My actions
My best foot forward defines me
My charm and intelligence
My confidence and fearlessness
Defines who I am

FIRE

These priceless characteristics aids in the
molding of what I am and where I am going
So respect what defines me

I am a unique kind of talent
The kind of talent that makes you develop two
kinds of love; either you love me… or love to
hate me
(*Smile*) But by all means it's your choice
Love me, Hate me
Appreciate me, Disregard me
Understand me, Judge me
But in the end you will know where I am
coming from and Respect the ingredients that
define me as the person you've come to know

Acknowledge me,
Recognize my abilities and who I am

You try to call my bluff
Try to define the real reason I come around
Don't speak on what you don't know your
beliefs ***DON'T MEAN SHIT!***

***I DON'T NEED YOUR DEFINITIONS OR
YOU TO RATE MY EXPERTISE***

***JUST KNOW I CAN SHOW UP AND SHOW
OUT!!! AND THAT'S SOMETHING I WILL
TELL YOU ABOUT!!!***

I am smooth with my presence
No cheap imitation

INDEPENDENT

I am electrifying with my words
and my performance is amazing

I am me
Your sharp tongue can't help influenced my
style
Honestly, I can care less if you like it or not
If you have nothing better to do define me if you
will, but I guarantee you what you get is *100%
REAL*

Define me and do your best giving your best
definition…

But to sum it up

I am Kaiserrific
And Kaiserrific is who I will remain to be
Respect me… period… cause this is me...for
who I was, who I am, and who I will be
So I assure you your negative definitions don't
mean shit to me… because at the end of the
day…I define me…

*For awhile it's always someone that
will not show you any respect. Question your
authority and your purpose from the minute
you come around. You have to introduce
yourself every now and then to let people know
that you mean business. I never called
anyone's bluff or try to figure why people want
to come around certain people. That's not me
and that's not what I define. You will get the*

FIRE

real deal out of me and anyone who tests me can step forward... I'm Kaiserrific and I can hold................my...............own.

INDEPENDENT

FIRE!!!

***WHY IS IT THAT MOTHERFUCKERS
ALWAYS TRY TO CALL YOU OUT?***
Then, when I tell them about their ass, they
want to sit and pout
Thinking they know any and everything and
don't know shit
Better watch it bitch or you get lit
You'll be on *FIRE, FIRE!!!*
My words are like *FIRE, FIRE!!*
Imma set yo ass on *FIRE, FIRE!!!*
***YOU'LL WISH YOU NEVER FUCKED
WITH ME!!***

Burn yo ass up in a matter of minutes
When I'm done with you, you'll be burnt like a
pot of grits
Once my fire gets to you, you'll be so toasty and
crisp
You'll be burned from the bottom to the top of
your lips
YOU'LL BE ON FIRE, FIRE!!!
MY WORDS ARE LIKE FIRE, FIRE!
IMMA SET YO ASS ON FIRE, FIRE!!
WHEN I GET DONE WITH YOU, YOU'LL
WISH YOU NEVER FUCKED WITH ME!!

I got a few words for all my enemies and foes
Every now and then I feed into you hoes
But Imma tell you without having to spit or spat
Listen to what I got to say and we'll be done
just like that

FIRE

KEEP FUCKING WITH ME THEN YOU'LL
BE ON FIRE, FIRE
IMMA SET YO ASS ON FIRE, FIRE!!
YOU'LL BE ON FIRE, FIRE!!!
MY WORDS ARE LIKE FIRE, FIRE!
WHEN I GET DONE WITH YOU, YOU'LL
WISH YOU NEVER FUCKED WITH ME!!

FOR THE ONES THAT BE IN MY FACE
LYING AND SMILING
Imma light yo ass up!
While I'm flaming yo ass up; you'll be
cryin'and cryin'
YOU'LL BE ON FIRE, FIRE!!!
MY WORDS ARE LIKE FIRE, FIRE!
IMMA SET YO ASS ON FIRE, FIRE!!

THE ONES THAT BE BRAGGIN' AND
FLOSSIN'
Your burnin' clothes you'll be tossin' and
tossin'
I'll be there sitting and stalling
You'll be asking someone to come save you is
what you'll be callin'
YOUR ASS IS ON FIRE, FIRE!!!
MY WORDS ARE LIKE FIRE, FIRE!!!
YOU STARTED THIS FIRE, FIRE!!!
WHEN I GET DONE WITH YOU, YOU'LL
WISH YOU NEVER FUCKED WITH ME!!

THE ONE THAT BE TALKIN' ALL SHIT
Better shut the fuck up before you get lit
You fucked with me and made this way

INDEPENDENT

Burning up in front of me is what you got to pay
YOU'LL BE ON FIRE, FIRE!!!
MY WORDS ARE LIKE FIRE, FIRE!
IMMA SET YO ASS ON FIRE, FIRE!!
YOU'LL WISH YOU NEVER FUCKED
WITH ME!!

WHAT ABOUT THAT BITCH FROM
ACROSS THE STREET?
Tells me she wants to feel my heat
Always talking trash
You just mad because I didn't want your ass!
YOUR ASS IS ON FIRE, FIRE!!!
LETTING YOU BURN UP WAS NOT MY
DESIRE, DESIRE!!!
BUT YO ASS IS ON FIRE, FIRE!!
WHEN I'M DONE WITH YOU, YOU'LL
LOOK LIKE ASHES!

TO ALL MY MOTHERFUCKING HATERS!
Imma tell you this now and later
It's all about my fire, fire!
I love that my words are fire, fire!
You can't touch me with my fire, fire!
Step one foot close to me and I light yo ass up!
I got that fire, fire!
Chicks know about my fire, fire!
Better warn yo boys about that fire, fire!
When I light you up, you'll never want to fuck
with me!!!

FIRE

TRASH TALK

Man look at Kaiserrific,
I wonder about him
You know they say about him
Yeah I heard this
I heard that
I wonder if it's true
I heard it from his cousin's baby momma
Yeah I know what I'm talking about
Wait, wait be quiet!
Here he comes…

Silence

You can sit in the bleachers to hide and make
me your small talk
Walking through the crowds having your petty
conversation
You can sit on the phone with your girlfriends
and gossip about me
I hear it, I know it, I smell it and I feel it

Don't think I'm in the dark not knowing what
you said
I hear you
I hear you
And I hear *YOU!*
You ain't got to turn back to say something
about me
When actually you been trying to scrutinize me
And I don't act like I don't see what you are
doing

62

INDEPENDENT

While you keep those false accusations going
and going
You trying to talk trash about me without me
realizing it
But you wrong I see it

What you don't think I know what you all are
saying?
In no kind of way am I playing
You don't think I know how you truly felt
Instead of what you said about me I rather been
beaten with a belt
With all the negative vibes going around, I'm
wide awake hearing it all!
Instead of people always putting me in lies
when I was never involved
Spreading all that trash talk, gossip talk
Spreading all your lies about me

They say he is gay
WHAT KIND OF SHIT IS THAT?
BETTER BE GLAD I DIDN'T JUMP UP
AND BEAT YO ASS WITH A BASEBALL
BAT!!!
LYING ABOUT SOMETHING THAT'S NOT
TRUE!!!
ATTEMPTING TO HURT MY FEELINGS
TO LEAVE ME BLUE!!!
AFTER I GET THROUGH FUCKING, YOU
BE LOOKING LIKE A FOOL!!!
HOW YOU GON KNOW IF YOU CHASIN'
DUDES THAT'S OUT OF YOUR LEAGUE?

FIRE

*YOU WISH YOU HAD A MAN LIKE ME
WITH ALL OF MY INTEGRITY
WHEN DUDES THOUGHT I WAS, I COULD
HAVE BEEN SLEEPING WITH YO
CHICK!!!*

I hear he talks to too many women
*YOU DON'T KNOW ME PERSONALLY TO
LET THAT COME OUT YOUR MOUTH!!
YOU JUST MAD CAUSE I'M NOT
TALKING TO YOU
MAD BECAUSE I WON'T GO OUT IN
PUBLIC WITH YOU
MAKE YOU FEEL SPECIAL
DEALING WITH YOU I WILL CATCH ALL
TROUBLE*

He is too nice and seems a little weird
*MAYBE IF YOU GET TO KNOW ME, THEN
YOU'D UNDERSTAND!!
WHAT? BECAUSE I DON'T ACT LIKE
YOU, THAT MAKES ME A NUISANCE?
I'D RATHER BE THAT THAN TO BE ONE
OF YOU BITCHES!!
I 'M CLASSIFIED AS THIS AND TAGGED
AS THAT
BUT YOU THE ONE WALKING AROUND
ACTING LIKE A RAT*

I'm supposed to be your friend
While you tell different lies behind my back
When you was the very one getting money for
laying on your back

INDEPENDENT

How could I ever trust you?
When I know you going to spread rumors about
me my family, my friends
Just like that chick that lied about her baby
being mines and tried to pull a Billie Jean on me

I am not going to waste my time on this
I already know what and who you are
You will be alright
I won't feed into your shit!
'Cause someone else will come along to get me
tangled in their spider web

TRASH TALKER, SCHEMING STALKER!
LYING TABLOID PIG, YOU TRULY MAKE
ME SICK!
I'M NOT WHAT YOU PEOPLE SAY I AM!
I STAND BEFORE YOU AND TAKE A
STAND!

Yet you can continue to talk trash about me
Until one day you know something interesting
about me
If you want to know something just ask
Don't sit and assume making yourself look like
an ass
Than to sit here and continue writing about your
negativity
I am going to get into some positive activity
Hearing about me in all of your lies
Attacking me in every one of your tries
Cause the lies and rumors that people will not
get to me

FIRE

The things you put out on me will not intimidate me...

INDEPENDENT

MONKEY BUSINESS (ALWAYS IN SOMEBODYS BUSINESS)

You see and know too much!
You keep your ear to the ground to hear too
much!
Always keeping my business in your mouth!
Trying to find ways to ruin and destroy my
name!
Putting me through all sorts of obstacles
People like you have tried to break my ground!
As always I find a way to turn it around!
I still overcame through it all

You had to be so nosey to witness all my
problems
The challenges that are a part of my life
You don't have any business of your own to
attend to
So you worry about mine and keep stirring up
trouble!
Exploiting my name associated with persuasion,
deception, and adultery!
To the very people that meant nothing to me
Spreading your lies and manipulations is your
monkey business!
Just to get your name recognized and spoken of

Then you want to spread my name all over the
web
You dirty, ratchet, inconsiderate asshole

If I was to be so ignorant to hang you up by a
tree
And set you on fire myself for attempting to
hurt me
But I'm going to let God handle you
'Cause everything you done to me is already
happening to you

For you to lie and say that I am homosexual
You really want your ass kicked and put in
order
You don't know shit about me you dirty bitch
Last time I checked you was the one getting
your ass fucked
Having your pussy ate by another chick
So who the freak now! Who's the pervert!

People cannot hurt me
But I can hurt them
Not with my fist, a gun, or a knife
But using the very weapons they used on me
Words and strong words that will seek out the
truth
The truth behind everything

Some of my relationships were broken because
of people and their cruel words
Them sticking their noses all into my business
and personal life
Not knowing anything but only what they heard
from all the haters
By her foolishness of listening to them
I overcame that when I found someone new

INDEPENDENT

It may have taken me long but she is here
And very well appreciated by me
No one I don't think want to stop this
But who knows, I must prepare
For I am not great and powerful
I am only a man but nothing can change that
But still I stand and continues to stand
Stand strong all over your face

(Originally written in 1999)

Chapter 3

REVELATION

(The Reality)

There's Nothing Realer Than Life!

REVELATION

4 DAYS

Concept to writing "4 Days"

In April 2010 I created "4 Days". This monologue was the creative compilation of trauma and reality. As a male sensitive to the plight of women, I have been privy to the innermost passions and pain of my many female friends and acquaintances. This privilege of witnessing such consequences as broken hearts and shattered dreams served to increase my respect and admiration for all women. That reverence for the experiences of women is what inspired me to write "4 Days".

In writing this monologue, I wanted something powerful that would touch people. I felt that women are survivors just like men and I wanted to reach out to all the women who have gone through spousal abuse of any kind. Be it mental, physical or verbal abuse; no woman should have to experience abusive treatment, especially not under the pretense of "love".

Some women are able to utilize their strengths and defend themselves emotionally, physically and mentally against their abusers, including taking steps to leave the relationship. For example my mother, though she was exposed to abusive men, she did not condone abuse. She fought back. But we have women who are not as strong or ready or fear for their actual

FIRE

lives. So in this story, I wanted to illustrate the character that was going through a horrible marriage, yet did not know how to get out of it. She was caught up in her feelings and was confused as to whether or not to leave or remain. This is her story...

(Whisper)
Look at her, do you know what you've done to her?

(Husband)
Man FUCK her! She ain't shit to me and she ain't NEVER going nowhere! I'm hers and she is mine! I'll KILL that bitch before she leaves me!

(Screams and is crying)
Ahhh! God! Will somebody help me!

(Day One)
I can't deal with this anymore! I've had enough!
I'm tired of going to the mirror everyday
looking at how swollen my face has gotten,
from him taking his large fist with rings and all,
plunging directly into my small fragile face.
I cannot continue spitting up blood in the
bathroom face bowl from when you busted my
jaws open, almost knocking out my teeth.

So you think it's okay to lay your hands on me
each day and every night 'cause you're my
husband?

REVELATION

You feel it's okay to do me so wrong, but I'm
wrong for letting you do these awful things to
me!
What kind of woman am I?
My mother taught me better than this.
She said never to be anyone's crutch.
I know people are wondering what is going on
with me.
Wondering why I have on shades when I'm
inside or at night?

I have to buy make-up and cake it up to hide the
bruises and scars you leave on my face.
You don't want me as your wife; you want to
use me as your punching bag!
You need to find someone else because I am not
the one anymore!
I refuse to take this shit anymore from you or
any other man.

So step off and leave me the hell alone!
You say that you are going to stop, 'cause you
love me.
If you love me, I wouldn't be in this situation.
I was once a beautiful woman and now look at
me!
I am a horrible masterpiece you have created!

(Day Two, six months later)
He hit me again and this time it got worse.
I can't believe he fucking dragged me all
through the house!
I can't believe his ass pulled half of my hair out!

Then you buy me a wig to hide the bald spot
where you pulled my hair out.
My stomach hurts from all the times you kicked
me in it, calling me a bitch,
Repeatedly, telling me that this is love and no
one else is gonna love me like you!

You had me screaming so loud when you raped
me, when I refused sex from you.
I didn't want to be touched by you because of
how you beat me…That turned me off!
So now I have no voice to speak to anyone not
even my momma.
You made sure that I wasn't going to talk to
anyone today or the next day after that!
You got your kicks off when you bashed my
head into the wall 15 times,
And I stopped counting after that 'cause I
blacked out on the kitchen floor.
You sit there laughing at me while I recover,
trying to patch myself up.

I never understood why when we're out with
our friends you are a totally different person!
You smile at me, trying to make me feel like I
was a million dollars to you.
You were flashing around this false love to
make people think that we are truly in love.
You are such a liar and I want people to know
the truth about who you really are!
Then you cuddle up in bed under me like
everything is ok between us.

REVELATION

You are such a bitch and I regret the day I
married you!

(Day Three, one year later)
He beat me again and damn near left me for
dead.
I swear that bastard broke my ribs with that
metal baseball bat!
The worse he drinks, the worse my beatings
become.
The more frustration in his life, the more he
tortures and hurts ME.
I feel sorry for him 'cause he can't get the
people that hurt him in his life.
Instead he don't feel sorry for me and I get the
worse kind of treatment.

I'm so mad at myself cause this bitch-ass man
broke my nose!
Then he had punched my eyes so badly to where
they are swollen shut!
He raped me again in the act of sodomy to the
point he tore all my insides up.
I was so in shock that this man, who SAYS he
loves me, would do this heinous act!
I am so ashamed that I know this man, but I am
scared to tell anyone.

The nurse at the hospital asked me to press
charges against him.
I made a vow but, why was I so stupid to let
these charges go?

I refused her help and as always accepted the beatings once again.
I know that I said I was not going to take it anymore, but…
Its hard and … (crying)…but I think I love this man, but do I?
Do I want to keep getting my ass kicked for the rest of my life?

God, I come before you to ask for help.
I cannot continue to remain in this abusive marriage.
This man says he loves me but he beats me daily and blames me.
He blames me for how his life was ruined.
But I been nothing but too good to him.
Please, dear Father, answer this prayer. Please Lord, in Jesus name. Amen.

(Whisper)
Why did you just walk up and smack her in the head with that belt while she's praying over you all's marriage?

(Husband)
Like I said, I don't have nothing to worry about cause she ain't going NO where!

(Day Four, one month later)
Today was different from any other day than before.
I left him…

REVELATION

Left him for good!
He never thought that I would be gone.
Oh but he is gone too…where he is going he
won't ever hurt another woman again!

He is going to get his payback.
I hope that he prays to God that the men in jail
don't kill him.
But, whenever he looks in the mirror and see
that huge scar on his face,
He **WILL** remember who put it there!
When he looks at the scars on his chest and
throat, he will immediately think of me!
I did put up a fight this time and fought with
every bit of my strength.

He went too far last night. He was high as well
as extremely drunk.
Yeah he went too far, snapped my neck and
killed me instantly.
I chose not to die without a fight!
This time I fought for all women who are going
through this shit, but I lost the battle.
But you'll probably win the war for all women
united!

As for him, I heard he got a life sentence
without parole.
When the police finally showed up he sat there
on the floor with me, bloody, in his arms crying.
With him smelling like he had been drinking for
days and high as a kite, he realized that I was

FIRE

not getting up, yelling repeatedly shouting "I'm
so sorry! I'm so sorry!"
It's too late now, I'm gone forever and it's on
him to thank.

As for me, I am being held by one of God's
Angels.
No more suffering and no more pain.
No more abuse.
I'm free!
I pray that none of you women ever end up like
me...

*(Originally written April 21-22, 2010. Later
performed on April 2 & 3, 2011 in
Edwardsville, Illinois at Southern Illinois
University.)*

*View the live performance of "4 DAYS" on my
website: kaiserrific.webs.com*

REVELATION

DEEP EXPOSURE
(UNDERNEATH THE MASK)

Ever had someone you spotted from a crowd of people that look so distinctive from everyone and you had to meet them? Once you meet them, you get to know that they are not as they appear to you for real. You later find out they are a totally different person, living a totally different life. To every person they meet, they are not as they appear. Change their looks, sound, living in different homes. They wear a mask that will never reveal the truth about them.

Tell me who in the hell you are!
Who are you?
What are you?
I don't know if I should like you
Love you
Or to even trust you
But you're always trying to get me to lust you
Then you get you mad if I don't fight you
Take off the mask to show the deep exposure of
who you really are

I am not sure as how to describe your identity,
You are an unusual woman to me
A distinctive looking woman to most men
A plain individual to everyone else
I bet you don't even remember what you
originally look like,

79

FIRE

You fooled yourself for so long to look and
sound like this person,
That you believe to become this other person
Or persons for that matter...

TAKE IT OFF!!!
TAKE OFF THE DAMN MASK!!!!
Remove the camouflage you been wearing for
so long.
Revealing the lies that you tell everyone else are
the condiments of that mask.
The lies and games that you play with me or any
man that you come across.
But you don't have to be someone that you're
not just to impress me.

You made me your business took a major
interest in me.
I found it very surprising and I was intrigued,
And without consideration and deep thought, I
opened my doors to see where it goes
But with the mask you were disguised which
changed my decision.
Full of deceptions, lies, manipulations!
You're cruel, you're wrong, you're deceitful,
you bitch!
You weren't who I thought you were!
So now my doors are closed for good
Cause you did it to me
To him, because he didn't accept you
To her because she was not for you
And to whomever that will fall for it
People that didn't do anything to you

REVELATION

You appeared to love me and value me as yours
Brought me into your home
To feed me, bathe me, caress me, and lust my
entire body
Made me feel like I was the only man you had
in your entire life
I was the king of your castle
How many men have you told that lie to?
Exploring your bisexuality like any other
woman
How many women have you brought into your
home?
How many times have you lied about ever being
with a man?
Lying to her, lying to him, lying to me
Lying to anyone that believes you
Not realizing that you are lying to yourself

Running changing your look every week
Changing your hair color to hide the original
root color of your hair
Buying new clothes, wearing the outfit but only
once
Switching cell phone carriers making limited
calls to certain people
Having numerous amounts of plastic and
cosmetic surgery
Caking your face down with that make up called
FAKE,
To hide every wrinkle, beauty mark, or
whatever is on your body
Changing your voice so you won't be identified

FIRE

Swapping cars every month from the rental
What are you hiding?

I see you continuously re-decorate your house
every chance you get
To make it hard to remember or notice this
place once before
When I lived here or any man that has lived here
In fact, many men lived here both past and
present
They knew you as a different name, different
face, and different attitude
Can you explain the different wigs in your
closet?
The different pictures of your look
All those glitches that keep playing back
Playing back everything you once were

Your former life
Your former loves
Your former way of living
Everything about you now is a lie
You hide behind the mask to direct your world

*SHATTER THE MASK! TRY TO COME
OUT OF IT!!!*
Remove the mask piece by piece
Reveal who you really are
Remove that plastic covering from your face
You're just like other people
You hide what's inside because you're not
happy with yourself
You're not happy with how you living

REVELATION

So you put on the mask

To read your story from your diary,
You were once beautiful
Could have been a model or the next Miss
America
Had everything you wanted and much more
Sharing a good life with someone you was
deeply in love with
One man came into your life and changed you
forever

Until one day,
He started saying you were ugly
Throwing you around the room
Blackening your eyes
Making you wear old torn up clothes
Not allowing you to comb your hair until your
hair came out

Kept you as his slave
Telling when you can come out the room and
who you can talk to
Making you cook all his meals
And if it didn't taste, he punch you in the mouth

So when attempted to make you pretty and he
didn't like it
He would do something to make you ugly all
over again
So one day you got real tired of the bullshit
So you poisoned him and he died of no known
causes

FIRE

No one ever knew you killed this horrible man
So you made a vow to yourself to never re-live
that again
So you always changed your looks
When men started doing things that mister did,
you eliminated them immediately
Before they get too further into you

So when the men started getting annoying
You would change your entire identity
So you could not be located
No contacts with them
No tracing you from a phone call, as to why you
change your numbers or carrier
Sending your mail going to a Post Office instead
of your home address

Collecting your money from your dead husband
that you killed
And making investments to produce more and
more money under various names
Just to live your life under the mask you walk
around in
Live another day to replace or as you may think
to cover the life you once lived
You've done this for years
But when you met me, you took a liking. You
had your moments with me
I was special to you because I can see beyond
what you have on your face
But I was not enough for you,
And you will never be honest with me

REVELATION

But I couldn't change you, even if it took the
life of me
You vowed to live your life in this mask

The mask is what you will wear
Throughout the rest of your life
A shell that will hide all of your emotions
Your fears no one will ever know
Your truest feelings only you will feel

You will continue to live as another person
Living another life in another world
A world you created for your protection
Having another lover everyday
Having another adventure with another group of
people
And like everyone else you continue to live
another life...

Deep exposure underneath the mask you will
always be...

DREAMS

We all have dreams
I have mine and you have yours
But I don't stop you from pursing it
So I ask that you don't stop me

I dream to climb mountains
You dream to have all the riches in the world
I dream to be famous and loved by millions of
people
You dream to win the lottery
Hmmm, our dreams are so based on different
feelings

I dream to spread love and peace throughout all
of humanity
You dream to lust every woman that you can get
your hands on
I dream to be one with myself again
You dream to be one with some girl in the back
seat of your car
I don't knock your dreams, so don't knock mine

I dream to dance like MJ and moonwalk all over
again
You dream to dance on poles to make a few
dollars
You say my dream doesn't mean anything
But I can't say yours mean anything as well
Dream a little dream with me…

I dream for a good life,

REVELATION

The one with the wife, kids, white picket fence
While you dream for drugs, alcohol, sex, and
groupies
I dream to have a woman that completes me
You dream to go from man to man finding one
quality in them that you can have in one man
But remember, dreams are made up by our
personalities
And our personalities are so different

Like my friend dreams of being a great singer
Yet he will continues to succeed at his gift
But the dreams of some of his associates
determine him to have failure
Because their dreams are not being fulfilled
It's not our fault you chose to walk another path
than his

Another friend dreams to succeed as a writer,
poet, and artist
Proven many times to have the potential to do
so
But you dream to hate on her 'cause you're not
the one to do the same thing
But your dreams are not hers, so step…
We can't always please the world
So quit trying to make our world your world

All my friends' dreams are made up of different
qualities
And nobody can come about to change them
We wouldn't change yours
So don't change ours

FIRE

Our dreams are the ideas that make up our
creative style
So don't hate on my dreams and I won't hate on
yours
You curious about my dreams…

Well my dreams are different than yours or any
others
My dreams are beyond my fantasies
Beyond my friends and beyond yours
Can you really handle my dreams?
I don't know, it's not like anything I ever
imagined.

My dreams are more than you could ever
possibly vision
I dream things beyond the ordinary
It could include you
It could include me
You'll never know

Dreams are the beyond words I come to know
about
Powerful dreams
Motivating dreams
Deep dreams
Dreams that the rich imagined having
Dreams that children set out to have
But my dreams are real
What's real to me may not be real to you
But these are my dreams…

But I won't tell you because it's my dreams…

REVELATION

ISOLATION (THESE 4 WALLS)

I sit here with these 4 walls in pure isolation
It's quiet and so peaceful doing its usual
dedication
Dedicating to making me feel so alone
Not to having anywhere to go
Nor having anyone to hang around
It's just me and these 4 walls

If these walls could talk,
We would have a lot of conversations discussed
Plenty of things to talk about
Share many laughs about this and about that
Believe me; they probably have stories about
the times before I came here
We'd probably be up all night
Or at least until I fall asleep

I am starting to believe that these 4 walls know
me better than most people
Know me better than my family
Any woman that I have ever dated
Anyone I went to school with or worked with
Better than anyone I met off the street in the
matter of minutes
Only because I felt like that's all I ever had was
the isolation with my sanity
My isolation was not anything that I requested
Nor did I ever give permission for it to come
around
Just came to me one day out of nowhere
With no money to go anywhere or to see anyone

FIRE

So these 4 walls kept me company for some
time now

So many rumors to my isolation have sum up all
to nothing
Some say that I am suffering from a depression
Due to not having a job
No love life with the right woman around
No life at all forreal and you know how people
desert you when your money leaves
Cause they don't want to pay your way if you
need it
Maybe it was my time to sit in the house and it
saved me from a lot of trouble I could have
gotten in
Or could have been that I didn't want to be
bothered with the outside
But who in the fuck really knows!

Maybe this gave me time to sort out my life
Sort out every thought that goes through my
head
Sort out who my true friends are
Sort out who were my true enemies
Plan out what my next move will be

But no one thinks about that
Always thinking of the worse in my favor
Can't ever be positive and good
I always get the worse happening to me
But people are going to be people

If I could talk back to the 4 walls,

REVELATION

I would tell everything that has been on my
mind so long
I would say exactly what I wanted to say for so
long
Walls if you can talk back please do so...

Sitting within those walls I would say,
HELP ME WALLS!!!!
I AM ALONE!
I AM WITHOUT LOVE!
WITHOUT A LIFE!!!
PEOPLE HAVE ABANDONED ME!
*PEOPLE WHO SAID THEY WERE MY
FRIENDS!!!*
*I AM WITHOUT AN EAR TO LISTEN TO
ME*
OR A VOICE I CAN LISTEN TO!!!

WITHOUT LIPS TO KISS ME!
WITHOUT A SOFT BODY TO TOUCH!!!
*WITHOUT THE MOTIVATION TO CARRY
ON!!!*
BUT I'M HURTING AND STRESSED!!!
*I CANT MOVE FORWARD TIL I GET THIS
OFF MY CHEST!!!*

*SO WITH THE STRENGTH OF GOD I
SHALL PROSPER!*
*I SHOULD BE ABLE TO CONTINUE TO
MOVE FORWARD!!*
BUT WHY DO I FEEL SO DOWN?
CAUGHT IN DIFFERENT MOODS!!
MY MIND IS PLAYING TRICKS ON ME!!

FIRE

GET IT TOGETHER!!!
I AM NOT DEPRESSED!!!!
I AM NOT HURTING!!!
IT'S TIME TO MAKE CHANGES!!
FINALLY REALIZE CHANGE IS FOR THE
BETTER!!
FOR ME AS WELL FOR EVERYONE
ELSE!!!!

I AM GOING TO DO RIGHT!!!
I WILL BE BIGGER THAN I EVER WAS!!!
I WILL ARISE BEFORE YOU EVEN KNOW
IT!
CLIMB BACK ON TOP!!!
SMASH ALL MY ENEMIES LIKE
ROACHES!!!

NO MORE BEING YOUR SIDEWALK!!!!
CAN'T WALK ALL OVER ME ANYMORE!!!
NO MORE OF THAT!!!
I AM NEW AND IMPROVED!!!
I AM NOT THAT PERSON YOU ONCE
KNEW!!!

WOOOOOOOOOOO!!!!!

But I am back in my isolated 4 walls
Sitting here all alone
But I am sitting here this time with a smile
I got everything off my chest
I feel so much better and relieved
I'm ready to face the world

REVELATION

I sat many days in my room and thought to myself about my next moves. I decided to write when I wanted to escape from anything that was bothering me. Writing has always been a big part of me and since I isolated myself I wrote things that best come related to me. At one point I thought so negative while walking with a positive mask on my face. Now, I am able to turn a negative situation into a positive situation. You can too! You must have faith with motivation to do whatever you want. You cannot allow others to block you from pursuing your happiness.

- Kaiserrific

FIRE

UGGGGHHHH!

UGGGGHHHH!
I don't want to wake up this morning knowing
that my daddy walked out on us again
Daddy felt that raising a family wasn't what he
wanted
Burnt out on us as usual when things are bad
and be back when we get situated and caught up
on bills and everything
Momma sells her body just to get enough for us
to eat,
Something that she is so against and tells us
every time not to make the mistakes she'd made
But having a momma at home sometimes is not
bad at all
Cause the thought of no momma at all could be
a lot worse
Like her choosing her man over us like some
moms do to seek love they've lost out on
Than to be a part of our lives to help lead us to
that better road in life

To go to school to be told by certain teachers
that we cannot become anything that we want to
be in our careers
How do they know that I will not become
anything of myself?
The education system only teach us their
history,
A history that is not anything that I can relate to
While my history only gets taught 28 days of
the 365 days of the year

94

REVELATION

And never hear about the successful black
people in African American History

Then to walk home in a neighborhood where all
you see are winos and drugs addicts standing on
every corner
Someone always walking up begging for spare
change or a few dollars
Every other day you see the police in the
neighborhood putting a sheet over another dead
body
Then afterwards, you never heard anything good
on the news about what the community is doing
Always hearing about someone robbing, killing
or dying at the scene of a crime
Children are always in the mix of someone
else's fatality
Either being raped, caught up in a gang war or
the shield of a shootout or...
Take their own life simply because they are
unhappy and feel like they will not be going
anywhere

UGGGGHHHH!
The government lies to each and every one of us
everyday
Telling us one thing and the next thing we know
it's something else
I'm tired of all these lies these rich politicians
tell everyday
You're not helping me, your helping yourself
make more money

Bring more money into your home to your rich
families
Then the one politician who is trying to help us,
People get salty and always disrespecting him
How can a man lead his country with no respect
from his citizens of this country?

The price of gas continue to rise, while the war
continues go on over oil rigs
People can't afford to get anywhere in their cars
or trucks
Taxes on food go up to where the cost of living
continues to rise
While I struggle asking anyone I know to
borrow some money
When I can be applying for a job but all the
good jobs been sent out of the country
No more opportunity unless you want to work in
a fast food joint

People don't think about how Congress stops
laws that the president been trying to pass
Then it makes him look bad
Then here comes these crooked wanna-be
politicians who want to say that America elected
a man that didn't know his job
When it was truly felt by certain people that we
had no business electing a black man in office
Feeling that a black man is not capable of
running an entire country
Especially when he has done more than what
these other so-called presidents have done for
anyone

REVELATION

If the blind-folded people continue to support
these rich politician wanna-be's
This country will go down and become a third
world country
It's going to take another strong experienced
educated person to bring America back on its
feet

UGGGGHHHH!
We have neither food nor hot water in my house
The system reduced my food stamps because
child support coming in the house
This is not enough to survive on for 5 kids and
myself under one roof
Energy assistance are not paying utilities right
now
I wouldn't have this problem if the electric and
gas companies didn't raise the amount
To help their companies make more money and
waste it on new buildings
When their headquarter buildings are in good
condition

Now I'm trying to figure out how to pay these
bills each month they are adding new changes
every minute
Then they don't want to help out with an
extension
But I see this man riding around showing off all
his money and fortunes
Able to drive down the street in a brand new
Cadillac
With tinted window and chrome rims

FIRE

Blasting all the damn beats in my ear and my
babies ear
That my poor babies have to hear waking up
wee hours of the night

Then get out of the car doing all of your loud
talking
Talking all that trash that nobody is interested in
hearing but yourself
You think it's ok to disrespect women right
outside my window
On my front lawn, making drug transactions in
front of my house
Having no respect for me or my children

Look here mister; I am single mother doing
what I can to provide for my children
I don't see anyone else entering my house
helping out
Making sure that kids are fed,
With the proper food to keep them healthy and
strong
Providing them with clean clothes everyday for
school
Getting up early in the morning to get them
ready and off to school
Nobody else teaching right from wrong
disciplining them after they did something bad
I don't need my babies to see all that garbage
you sell and smoke
Don't need the idea that it's okay to sell drugs
for a living

REVELATION

So I ask you nicely to please stop disrespecting
my household

Why don't you go get a real job?
One with benefits
Make something out of your life
Besides being a drug dealer
A woman abuser
The biggest show off in the neighborhood
When you're really the biggest ass!
A disrespectful human with no home training
I ask you now to stop before I get the police
involved
Then you wouldn't really like me
Thank you and have a good day!

UGGGGHHHH!
I am tired of working these petty jobs
Tired of living from pay check to pay check
No recognition for the work that I do to help
save this company
The only people that get recognized are the head
honchos that don't do anything
Taking every bit of credit for something they
had nothing to do with
Easily move up in the company kissing the
entire ass in the world
While I still sit here in this cubicle slaving a
computer for hours at a time

The more work I do for this company,
I feel the more I should be paid with benefits
and all

But that's too much like right so I am suppose to
be underpaid for my dedication
Having me sit in all these different training
classes to be only paid $7.50 an hour
Then sit in a meeting telling me that they can't
pay us more money
Because business is not coming in like they
were expecting
I sure can't tell the way I answer more phones
than any other agent on the floor

While other jobs they pay $15.00 an hour with
benefits
Those tend to be not surviving jobs
So quick to lay off cause they hired more than
what they need
Keep who they want and then bring in more
people at later season with a less hiring pay
This cycle keeps going round and round year by
year
But that's a bunch of bull cause I notice how
these executives buy all these new cars
Hearing about their new homes with the latest
furniture
Able to have breakfast, lunch and dinner at all
the classy restaurants
But continue to say that the company doesn't
have the money to pay more
Tell that to someone who got dumb ass written
all on their forehead

But when we do a good job for the company
they're so quick to reward us with some pizza

REVELATION

And it be the same people sitting up eating the
pizza thinking that company is really
appreciating them
Shoot the money you put into buying pizza
could have been a nice little raise on my
paycheck
Am I supposed to be grateful for the job that I
do have even though some are without one?

But why have a job when I can have a career?
Why work to get a few dollars here and there
When I can make so much a year doing
something that I love
Instead of something that I am doing just to get
by
It may be good for some people who feel this is
the American dream
But for me, having an investment in a career of
my choice
Will be a much better pay off

UGGGGHHHH!
Why do I deal with his same bullshit when he
got another woman?
I shouldn't want to be second to no other
woman anyway
I thought I was important to him since I was the
main focus of his life
He felt that my skin complexion was too dark
for him
Felt that he could not take me out in public
'cause he was ashamed

So he went out to get a much a lighter skinned
woman
I need to move on and find a man that will love
my beautiful chocolate skin
So hard for a good woman to find a good man
Just like looking for a good job
Ain't none around to go apply for or should I
say get with
Not be chosen based off complexion or color
Or judged cause I am not light enough to be
seen in public
It's the same vice versa don't settle for a piece
of a person
I feel chocolate women have a lot going on
Light skin women do too
It's no difference with us ladies
But if he wants something I'm going to let him
go
No begging to stay
Or asking to come back

That's that made up mentality created by the
racist society
Saying that anything light is better than dark
But that has changed
A change for the best
Go on ahead find what you were looking for
Let me be and be on about your business

My friend has it hard cause men overlook her
cause she is a full figured large woman
Only make her out as an object of sex
And she stops them right in their tracks

REVELATION

They get mad and want to talk about her weight
calling her a fat bitch
And she lets them have it with swollen lip for
disrespecting her

She truly loves herself no matter what
So what if she got more meat on her body
I love her and how she looks
Only a dog wants a bone
Believe me, it's a lot of dogs running around

But back to these tired ass men
I want better and if you can't come correct step
off!
Ugggghhhh!
(Man steps up whispering a bogus pick up line)
Didn't I just say come correct?
People make me wanna scream!

Ugggghhhh!

FIRE

Y

Why did you allow me to wake up this
morning?
To wake up to another story on the news about
someone dying
Crashing airplanes into two story buildings with
innocent people in both the buildings and planes
Then it's more killing in war or gang wars or
just because…
Why do you allow me to live and view such
violence?

Why do you allow young ladies to be corrupted
by the evils of men?
Taught to accept valuables in exchange for a
piece of their bodies
Why do some mothers, grandmothers, aunts,
uncles, and fathers teach them this is ok?
Why do you break the hearts of men that want
you for more than just your body?

Why do men enter in women's lives and corrupt
them because they want some ass?
Why do you feel it's okay to disrespect the
ladies in any shape, form or fashion?
Do you think it's okay if women treat you the
same way?
And I get caught on a hinge for the mess ups
you left behind

Why do some women allow men to beat on
them?

REVELATION

To respond saying "It's cause he loves me that
he does this."
Why do you call it love when it's physical
abuse?
To love someone is to cherish and care for them
instead of blacken their eyes
Why do some women feel that they have to feel
less of a woman in order to seek love?

Why do we live in a world where it's full of self
hatred?
Is it me or is it you that is the problem?
Why can't we get along using the simplest
things?
The simplest things that no argument or fights
needs to break out into
Why am I caught in the middle of race wars
going all the way back to yesterday?

Why do we live in such a world that we are
being judged?
You know people are going to live the life they
want to live
Do the things that they so much want to do?
It's not up to me nor is it up to you
So let it be and go on with your life

We live in a society where we cannot be the
person we want to be
Why?
Why do I have to pretend to be someone else to
please you or the next person?

FIRE

Why do some people try the hardest to fit into
society knowing they are not accepted?
Why is the world made of different colors,
shapes, and sizes?
Why did God create the world to be so
different?

Why do some black women have shapes and
curves?
Why do some black women have big plump
breasts and well rounded asses?
Why do you think rap stars always go for the
black thick chicks with body?
Do you think what you have enhances music
videos?
Why do white girls think it's cute to have a
super slim waist?
With no ass or breast at all
Do you think this will turn some men on at all?
Nothing to grab or to pull on or to even feel
We were all made for different reasons

Who said that when a boy become of a certain
age that your voice had to be deep?
Not everyone is going to sound like Barry White
or Melvin Franklin from The Temptations
How come we can't have voices of all different
sounds?
I like it that everyone sounds different even if
they sound like Michael Jackson

Why do some people think if you grew up tall
you suppose to be a basketball player?

REVELATION

Or because they're black they already know
how to play football or basketball?
Just because I'm tall or black doesn't mean I
have to be an athlete
Why do some black men have a large penis?
And want to go fuck everything that they see
Why do some white men think they can get
away with oral versus intercourse?
You think you can't win a woman over by not
using your penis so you use your tongue.

Why do some women think cause they have a
pussy they can get away with anything?
Just because you can open your legs and give it
up to get what you want, is not cool
See some states are in the favor of the woman
and behind closed doors the very ones screwing
the men that make the laws
Do we have to screw a woman in the
government to get some justice done?

Why do some women go for men that have all
the flashing cars, jewelry, clothes or whatever?
Instead of the men that can capture their heart in
the most unusual way
Do I need to have the bling bling to get your
undivided attention?
Why do some men look for women to pick up
where their mommies left off?
Expecting a woman to cook, clean, and take
care of you just like your momma use to

FIRE

Why do some women think that men suppose to
be always so masculine and tough?
Why can't he be sensitive and loving?
I don't see some of the ladies always being
feminine and soft
Why is it that some women want to be so
independent?
That leads to my next why question…

Why do some lesbian studs want to walk around
portraying the role of a man?
But when a fight breaks out with a man, she
runs to back that woman role real quick
And so quick to say that he ain't suppose to be
fighting a woman
So which are you going to be a woman or a
stud?
Now question to the femmes out there, if you go
and get a chick that looks and sounds exactly
like a man
Use a strap on and everything inserting inside of
you just like a man
Why not go and get a man?
You still get all the benefits… But I don't mean
to offend any of you

The same goes for men, if you want to penetrate
a man in his butt
While the other man call it boy pussy
To go after another man that is looking and
portraying a woman
Why not go and get a woman?

REVELATION

As for those men that looks and dresses like the
female
Why do you go after straight men?
When you're trying to screw him when you
portraying the woman.
Why not have another gay man? At least you
will be with someone that has a bond with you

Makes me wonder…
Why gay men who want to be women were not
born women?
Why lesbian women who want to be men were
not born men?
I think if they were born the sex they wanted to
be, they would still be attracted to the same sex.
Some questions were not meant to be answered
but again I don't mean offend anyone

Like politics, why do we have a divided
function of politics?
Why are republicans not for the common
American people but for the rich?
Why is it that when a democrat is fighting to
gain the vote to help the American people, the
very people that need to be out voting don't
show up?
Why do politicians say that when they get in
office, they will do everything to help you the
American people?
I haven't seen anything these politicians have
done yet

On a much sadder note,

FIRE

Why do young children or children period suffer
from abuse?
When they haven't harmed anyone
Then their minds are all messed up and will
never be the same
And cannot return to a normal life in the society
we live in
I am sorry babies for all you've been through

Why our elderly people are not properly taken
care of?
Then they die feeling like they were not loved
nor cared for
I am sorry for feeling like that and having to live
the rest of my life with that burden
People have to remember that one day; it might
be one of them in a nursing home alone,
Brokenhearted feeling unloved and unwanted

*So I walk through the city while it's raining, I
wonder about life, the way things are and what
they are. All I can only say is why?
Immediately questions start running through
my brain like the rain running down my
clothes, hair, and the sewer drains... God has
a plan to all the questions in my head and will
one day answer me...Why?*

Chapter 4

EMANCIPATION

(Freeing Yourself from Love's Heartbreaks)

Saying you Love Me, and Actually Loving Me are Two Different Things!

ALTERED ATTITUDE

Attitude #1
What the fuck is wrong with you?
I didn't sleep with you last night
You need to get it together
That's your motherfucking problem!
Yo stank attitude will not get us anywhere

I go to work to make a damn way for us
And your ass is never satisfied
Why the fuck are we still together?
I am tired of your ass
And you're tired of me too
This attitude has to stop!
We are so much better than this and you take it
so much for granted

With that altered attitude of yours
Will never keep me
Will never keep us as one
Will never keep us on the same path
Will never be the same between us

An altered attitude will destroy you
Destroy your love life
Your social life
Your family life
Your life period
And yet you don't give a fuck
WE'LL I DON'T GIVE A FUCK TOO!

Attitude#2

EMANCIPATION

Fuck these tired ass hoes
Tired of hoes always trying to control me
You can't control me and I ain't trying to
control y'all stupid asses
So don't fuck with me!
I got too much shit on my mind to be worried
about you all
You drama having bitches that keep shit going
on in your everyday lives
***GROW THE FUCK UP AND DO
SOMETHING PRODUCTIVE!!!***

I work and I provide for me and mine
I never ask you for shit
I have an altered attitude because you want to
judge brothers that are doing something for
themselves
Then when we get on our feet
You criticize us for that
For wanting something more than what we
already have
But some ladies want a man that don't do
anything for them
Who don't care about their families?
So easy to give mad love to the dudes that ain't
doing shit for their kids
Taking care of other women's kids that ain't
their blood
Say that we are selfish and we can be
I don't owe you a motherfucking thing
You need an altered attitude adjustment

With that current attitude of yours

FIRE

You will never have me
Will never keep me
Will never be on the same track
Will never be the same between us

An altered attitude will not destroy you
Save your love life
Your social life
Your family life
Your life period
But yet you don't give a fuck
WE'LL I DON'T GIVE A FUCK TOO!

Attitude #3
You think you know me but really you don't
You have me all figured out but haven't
You have me mapped out to my next move
But you don't know shit about me!

Yes I have an attitude
With damn good reason as to why I have one
But one day you're gonna learn
Going to learn that you can't figure me out by
certain actions I make
Take your fucking time. Quit rushing to know
all my juicy details
All things will come in due time

It's not always best to know something about a
person first hand
You learn a person by spending time with them
Talking with them
Laughing with them

EMANCIPATION

Not exploiting their personal business
You nccd to have an altered attitude...

With that current attitude of yours
You will never have me
Will never know me
Will never be on the same page
Will never be the same between us

Your unaltered attitude will destroy you
Won't save your love life
Your social life
Your family life
Your life period
But yet you don't give a fuck
WE'LL I DON'T GIVE A FUCK TOO!

(*Your conscience is speaking to you*)

You wonder why you're single
You wonder why you're not happy
You wonder why you're not where you want to
be
Wonder why you cannot move on with your life

It's simply you...
It's always been you
You the one that runs people away
You the one that makes you unhappy
You need to alter your attitude

Change your way of thinking
Change how you approach people

FIRE

Change to better yourself with others
Because of that attitude you possess you won't
ever change

You'll always be bitter and lonely
Be unhappy
Unsatisfied with yourself
Unsatisfied with anyone that will come into
your life

I'm coming to you because you won't listen to
anyone else
So if you heard from me, then maybe you might
just open your eyes
Open to an altered attitude
Change for the best
You got your life to live for
With the attitude you have, you will never get
any further...

***REAL TALK...GET AN ALTERED
ATTITUDE...***

EMANCIPATION

FUCK YOU LUV!!!

What do you really have to offer me?
NOTHING!
You have caused enough trouble already!
Look at the tears running down my face
Know how miserable I am when I walk around
people
Think about how I have to deal with the
realization of being single

Fuck you love!
You've been the biggest downfall in my life
The only benefits I ever got from you was pain,
Heartache,
A real fucked up mood of insecurity
And bad sex; rebound sex for that matter
And you would think that I would have been
treated better

Tell me what a person has to do to get some
quality time!
Affection!
Great foreplay!
A good cuddle right after some mad passionate
sex!
Do I have to place an ad in the want ads?

Fuck all the supporters of love!
Showing you all's public displays of affection
And your quality time together at the movies
With your silly lines of I love you baby and do
you love me?

FIRE

Why don't the birds sing in my window
anymore?

Love can kiss my ass!
You know what love, kiss your own ass!
I don't want you
But I did once need you
And I hurt sometimes because I don't have you
But it's ok, you don't have to like me or love
me!

But remember me
Remember when I was once in love
Remember who made me fall in love
The one that loved me unconditionally
Who made it so right when I thought it could be
so wrong
Remember I was once loved...

EMANCIPATION

I DON'T CHASE WOMEN, I DON'T KISS ASS AND I DON'T GIVE IN

What!
Am I suppose to run after you,
After the umpteenth time you have rejected me!
I've seen way more women to go after than you.
Women like you come every now and then.
And just because you look good don't mean I
got to be all over you.

Look at you!
Materialistic objects do not make you any better
than the next woman.
Some women don't have to do a lot to get my
attention
Plus you don't get too far with that materialistic
superficial attitude
If a woman wants me, then she knows how to
get me
But she ain't using her body to impress me
She uses her mind and her conversation to
express to me

I don't chase women, I don't kiss ass and I don't
give in
If you ever know me then you should know that
If not, I guess your left out in the dark
And I am not the one to give you a flashlight to
help you find your way

I feel that when you come to a certain point in
life where you stop chasing,
You don't have to do it anymore
I left that up to the young boys who are still
learning about women
As for me, I am a man and I know my role
I know what I have to do to get a woman
With what I know I have had my share

What you're talking about won't get me to like
you any better
If you're real with me in person,
Be real with me in public
No need to put that mask on pretending to be
someone you're not
I like the real women who are out here
I love the authentic woman that has her own
style and does not imitate another
I admire the genuine woman that acknowledges
and appreciates her man
I need a bona fide chick in my life forever
A true ride or die chick!
KEEPING IT REAL IS 100% COOL WITH
ME!

I don't chase women:
Why do I need to follow behind you?
Why would I need to go out my way to get your
attention?
Why do you think it's important that I get you to
notice me?
I don't understand you if I have to do all of that.

EMANCIPATION

I don't kiss ass:
Why would I need to kiss your ass to get
involved with you?
What would I get from this entire ass kissing,
what…a thank you?
You really want me to be all on you because
your built with the body parts I like
Guess again, I can get that from anywhere and
you ain't the only one.

I don't give in:
If I gave in to you, what becomes of it?
You think you've won over me
You feel like you have me putty in your hands?
I don't know what planet you come from but I
ain't the one.

SO NOW THAT YOU GOT THE RULES…
Here is what I'm telling you
The moral of this piece is blunt but simple,
That just because you think you're the shit,
And you did not smell the roses correctly
Don't mean your ass really is the shit
NOT THE TOP BITCH IN THIS PIECE!!!

You can plaster your face with all kinds of
makeup,
Weave your hair all you want and you'll still
have that after we break up
You can get your boobs all pushed up and make
your ass look full and firm
Thinking you the shit with that tired ass old
perm

121

FIRE

Wearing the skeetest dress to make you look
like you got a for real body
Knowing you look sick, would you like for me
to make a hot toddy?
But forreal you don't get my attention
I don't need fake or artificial, I need the natural,
the beautiful and the most real
There are plenty other woman in this world that
I can get with
And let's face it you're not one of them!

*I have had all sorts of women that
approached me and with certain qualities that
I liked. But when you come at me in the wrong
way like I am suppose to be all over you, I turn
the other cheek. It doesn't take a lot for me to
appreciate a woman. Like my sisters who are
real with themselves and real with who they
are make my day. I know that I will find true
love in them than the ones who are stuck on
the latest shoes, clothes, or etc. I still say I
don't chase women, I don't kiss ass, and I
don't give in… Can't make a man fall for you
'cause of who you are and if you're not, that's
good.*

- *Kaiserrific*

EMANCIPATION

MICROWAVE EFFECT

I sit up everyday hearing you microwave bitches
talk shit
Talk about how you want him to do this and do
that
Make sure he has your hair and nails done
Make sure he got your bill money for the week
And sad thing is you don't even know him at all
A complete stranger you met off the street last
week at $2 Tuesday

You all act just like a microwave, so instant and
quick to do something with a man
And yet you didn't have shit when you came
into the relationship
You are some foul bitches too
I never heard or seen no shit like this
What happened to taking your time to know a
person?
*NAW, YOU BITCHES BE ON THAT
"RIGHT HERE AND RIGHT NOW
SYNDROME"!
YEAH, I CALLED YOU ALL
BITCHES...BECAUSE YOU ALL ARE ON
BITCH MOVES!!!*

The minute a man opens his mouth, the first
question you ask him what his credit score is
Look him up and down giving him that eye
Then checks out what kind of job he has; what
kind of car does he drive

FIRE

Leading up to asking how many children does
he has and if he still with the mother
Before we know it you ask him who he lives
with
I'm not surprised if you bitches go home and do
a background on the net
Then expect to be engaged to him after 2
months of dating
If not married, make sure he puts an expensive
ring on your finger
You just like a microwave, turn your ass on for
5 seconds and you're on a mission
Missions to get what you want and do what is
necessary to go about getting it
Doing everything in the matter of seconds
Performing that instant oatmeal effect huh, well
you bitches got life all wrong

I remember when women took their time
knowing a man
Going on dates, meeting their families, and
occasional talks on the phone
What happen to the sit downs at the table and
talk?
Men learn about women by her conversation
and her actions
But since you want to drop the draws on the first
night I guess it tells a lot about you, huh?
Well you microwave hoes got another thing
coming

I keep using the term microwave meaning that
you're instant, quick, and fast

EMANCIPATION

Not too willing to take your time like a
conventional oven
Now besides women that are microwave
bitches, we have men who are microwave hoes
too
Be so quick to pull their penis out to give it up
to a woman they don't know shit about
Then, they finally realize they had no business
being with that woman in the first place

Some men go for a woman with a brain that
knows how to use it
With an established home that maintains to keep
all her utilities paid
Knows how to cook, clean and can hold down
her own to be a woman
But some dudes see pussy and $$$ and still
haven't learned anything about her
Accepts her gifts, her pampering, and fights
with her emotions that she puts on him
And you think that cause you laying the pipe
and giving it to her good
Feeling that's going to save everything you two
have in this "relationship"
Then applying your power of persuasion to get
any and every thing you want
But I notice this microwave effect happens to
just about anyone these days

People sometimes rush into things and not
realize what they're getting into

125

FIRE

Men desire a piece of ass so bad, do whatever
they can to get it and end up with a drama
queen, serial killer, or better yet burned
Some women are so quick to ask for some
money upfront because they feel like their
bodies are a product and demands to be paid for
it
So make a man pay for it and he hardly knows
ya
Later she comes to find out that he has another
family on the other side of town
And you was just an every now and then piece
for an instant climax
Then she wants to feel like she got mistreated
But if she gets instantly pregnant and he
instantly losing interest in her
Next thing you know, he's gone just that fast
Now as mothers, you shouldn't take your anger
out on the baby because the daddy didn't want
you
But you were acting like a quick fix for him to
get what he wanted
Then he is giving you some income for the next
18 years of your child's life

Brothers you knew better than to jump into a
situation with a woman you hardly knew
But you were being a microwave hoe or instant
bitch out to get the goods
Now you walking around with no money 'cause
of all your kids that instantly popped up
Not able to work a well paid job or have a life
that you so desire

EMANCIPATION

Then you want to blame that woman for all of it
But if men kept their penis in your pants instead
of so instantly pulling it out the minute she open
her legs then you all wouldn't be having these
issues
She might knew the plan the minute you walked
in the door
An instant trap to get the money

The microwave effect is a dirty motherfucker
And all you bitches, male and female, fall right
into it
You all want something right then and there
So quick to jump into a relationship, marriage,
or sexual relations
And don't know them from a can of paint

Take the time to know a person
Learn about who they are
Not about what they got or how they can benefit
you
Don't be so quick to microwave your entire life
fast
Then it won't be anything to enjoy in your later
years

Ah shit! Got to go, my soup is done
overcooking in the microwave!

PSYCHOPATH BITCH!

You the motherfuckers I do not want to deal
with
You take the world for granted for its little
advantages
You steal from the poor, to make more money
for the rich
You disrespect yourself in the most indecent
exposure
You ain't nothing but a psychopath bitch and I
hate you

You had to run to the child support services
because the daddy wasn't giving you enough
money to help raise your child
Then your dumb ass looks stupid when the
DNA test came back saying it wasn't his baby
You know how to make the nicest person turn
into the most evil human being on earth
I don't blame that man for whipping your ass in
front of all of your friends
Now your bitch ass gotta pay back all that
money of $5,000.00 to that man

Look at you psychopath bitch ass nigga and
yeah I said nigga
You had no damn right to go to that woman's
house and beat her ass
Even though she gave you genital herpes on the
first night of fucking
That still does not count for that woman to have
a black eye

EMANCIPATION

Then exploit her body and name all over the
neighborhood labeling her as a whore
You psychopath bitch ass nigga was a whore for
fucking her on the first night not knowing a
damn thing about her

You psychopath bitch ass motherfucker,
I ought to come kill your ass for what you did to
that nine month old baby
Sodomizing that little baby girl while her
momma was gone to work
You are a sick bastard that needs help and I
hope society punishes you with death
Give me a gun and I will shoot you myself

What about you two psychopath bitches, you
both were in the wrong of each other
How the fuck you think that no one would know
that you fucked her
She is only 14 and you are only 35
And how you thought he was going to stay in
your life by saying you're pregnant
Now he is gone now and left you with a six
month old baby to deal with
And you now locked up for statutory rape

Yeah mofo you won't ever mess with a
youngin'
They'll keep bringing you back to jail
Until it's too late you'll end up having
something
But lesson learned from all of this
You won't mess with young chicks

FIRE

I can't stand a psychopath bitch like you
To keep shit stirring up between families,
friends, or even loved ones
All because your silly ass is miserable and you
want some company
Go out and find some business, you crazy bitch
Make a new day for yourself
Quit being all over yourself
My family will be just fine
Once we pull you out of our bloodline

A punk pussy nigga like you to make me and
my son have a distant relationship
You just mad cause you'll never get any of my
attention
Make you feel important
Allow you to have control over me
But that's too fucking bad
Go the store and buy some fucking Glad
Ain't got time for this shit
I am not taking it in one bit
Bitch be gone
Now I can sing my song

**BITCH BE GONE! YEAH! BITCH BE
GONE!! YEAH!**

Or what about you, you psychopath excuse of a
man
You think it's alright to fight your wife right
after she had surgery

EMANCIPATION

To fight her in front of her young children, then
having their mama locked up
Then come back and took everything they had
money, food, etc.
Now you're suffering in your later years 'cause
of how you treated her

To go through your child's entire life by
verbally abusing him
Putting him down so bad when he already had
people putting him down from a child to an
adult
Instead of being a father to him, you became his
worst enemy
Instead of encouraging and bringing him to be
right
He is now an adult, yet you still try to dictate his
life
Watch the things he do, the people he got
coming around

You act like you're jealous and feel you gotta
keep up with him
But you never want to see him come up in life
to have something
You only selfish about all of your wants and
needs
But your time is slowing down as you get older
But when you realize that you are completely
shut out from what he does
Once he leaves, you won't have anybody
You'll be a sad old man before you realize it

FIRE

Tired of all you psychopath bitches
Always throwing me into your glitches
Always saying this and saying that
If I had it my way, I would beat your ass with a
baseball bat
YOU PISSING ME OFF!
KEEP FUCKING WITH ME I WILL SHOW
PEOPLE THAT YOU AIN'T NOTHING BUT
SOFT!!!

I'm with this and that's the end
You'll always be my enemy and never my
friend
It's cool and that's how it ought to be
I'm so through with you that I set you free

There are always going to be people
that will make you angry when you least expect
it. It would be much better to be cordial and go
on about your business. However, sometimes
you just want to knock someone upside the
head every now and then. But let's keep down
the violence and bring up the peace...

- *Kaiserrific*

EMANCIPATION

SCORNED

I am hurt and tired
Tired of opening myself up to you
I give my love, my heart, and my soul
AND I GET STRUCK DOWN WITH
HEARTACHE!

I am tired of crying my heart over you
I cannot live my life like this
You hurt me and later I hurt others
You only love when you want to hurt me more

YOU DON'T REALLY LOVE ME!
You never did to begin with
It was an excuse to get closer to me
To use and abuse me

Abuse my trust, honesty, and commitment
WELL GET THE FUCK OUT OF MY LIFE!
BECAUSE I DON'T NEED YOU!
SURE IN THE HELL DON'T WANT YOU!
YOU'RE SO FULL OF SHIT!

How dare you come back into my life?
You only wanted to fuck me
But instead you got me pregnant
Now I am taking care of this child by myself

Yeah while you was out with your hoes
I sat around and carried our baby
For 9 months and took care of us,

FIRE

All by myself and I didn't ask or need your
money of any kind for support

Now your broke ass come around
Now that my baby is old enough to speak
Don't you tell my child your entire stupid ass
lies!
Lies about why we were not together
I didn't have you around as the father
***MY CHILD SURE IN THE HELL DOESN'T
NEED YOU NOW!***

I am a strong woman and it's going to remain
that way!
From now until the day I die
DON'T TRY TO KISS ON ME!
STAY THE FUCK AWAY FROM ME!
Don't think you can come back whenever you
want like it's ok
Telling me that you love me
But my friends saw you with some other chick
on your arm
What the hell is wrong with you?
Don't you get that through your big ass head of
yours?
That I don't want you
Never do want you ever
Stay with your hoe and her child!
Where you can be called Daddy
And have your little family
Because there ain't no family for you here
You've messed that up a long time ago

EMANCIPATION

(Originally written "MAMA'S DRAMA"
November 28, 1999)

FIRE

SMOOTH TALKER

I love the way that I move into your heart
Capturing the things that you kept away from
other men
Getting you caught up in your feelings
Expressing your secrets to me that you never got
to tell the man that you were previously in love
with
Persuading you to give me your body
Grabbing your full focus and undivided
attention
Smoothing out all the hard surfaces you kept
from men
And again I've gotten into places where other
men haven't
It only took a matter of conversation and trust

I woo you and you didn't even realize it
I make you feel things that your boyfriend or
husband wouldn't thought of to make you feel
I am so good at it
I got you all over me
It didn't take much to do
I didn't have to use a magic formula
I only use the main ingredient that always works
Not my sweet charm
Not my significant amount of lust
But being who I am
I got you completely in love with me
Now you can't get enough of me

EMANCIPATION

So infatuated it's not anything that you won't do
for me
You devoted your life to me
Giving me everything that is a part of you
Immediately placing me into your life
The keys to your car, I got it
A key to your home, I got it
Your ATM card, you place in my possession
Showering me with all sorts of unexpected gifts
While you sneakily slip money in my pants
pocket
Making me feel truly special
Trusting me with your life
And I do what I do best, love you

Smooth Talker, Smooth Operator, Ladies Man,
Flirt, Playboy
Are some of the names that you all call me
Come into your life with a blink of an eye
Making good feelings you kept back from
everyone else come alive
Make you feel like you're on top of the world
You tell me over and over that I am the man of
your dreams
Because I make you feel like the woman of my
every desire

I am not hard to find
You might find me in a crowd of people
Might see me on the street by myself
See me out with other women
I am so smooth and so quick about how I do
things

But you won't have me caught up
You will never figure me out as you all have
tried on other men

I'm so smooth that my techniques can't be
traced
I'm not a ladies' man
But I am a flirt
I could never be a playboy
So don't try to pull a fast one on me
I knew the game and ran with it a long time ago

While I'm wooing you
I woo her
She is wooing me
Next thing you know I got women all over me
I just smooth talk my way into any woman's
heart
Make her feel above the clouds
And I sit back loving what I do best
Make a woman feel like she is the world
I love having a woman all in my arms
Lets me know that I am doing my job right

I can woo any woman that comes into my
existence
I woo your friends
Your sisters
Cousins stop to take interest in me
I can't help who I am
I love who I am….a smooth talker

Work my magic on you by one kiss

EMANCIPATION

One touch with my hands
One look that gets you all wet
One thing that comes out my mouth

I smooth talk around to get the missing
condiments in my life
Love, fun, pure pleasure, and the company of a
woman
Yes, I meet different women
Know different women
Learn different women and their characteristics
Only so I know how to approach them with my
smooth talk

I'm just a smooth talker
Here one day, gone the next
Go to sleep with you wrapped in my arms
And you wake up to a pillow in my place
Smoothness of how I do things
Cause I'm a smooth talker

THE BEAST WITHIN
(YOU MADE ME WHAT I AM)

As dark clouds rise, my spirits fall
The very last days of my life has turned around
I am no longer your companion, friend or even a
lover
I am no longer the ear to hear your voice speak
on such things
You ruined everything that you had with me and
could have had much more
But you blew it and only you are to blame for
all of this

I am now a blood thirsty beast, ready to take
your soul from you as you've taken from me
See I was nice, but you all killed me in broad
daylight
Felt like a swift stab in the back with your knife
made of deceit
Or better yet a gunshot coming from your 12
gauge made of heartache
Killed me with your deceptions, lies, and
manipulations
Your misused ways, abusing my deepest
trait...my kindness

I can't do that anymore for you or anyone else
Don't call me when trouble lurks again
I'm not your Captain Save-a-Hoe
I'm not your crutch to lift you up again

EMANCIPATION

Then you beat me with it the very minute you
are on your feet

I am tired of your excuses and hot air balloon
talk
You're going to say this and do that
And again you're going to take him back
You go back to the one that has your heart
The very one that destroys your soul once the
relationship is over

As for you, you can sit there and comb your hair
Look in the mirror; notice how you look so
perfect and so right
You can distinguish all over to people how cool
you are
You claim you're a diva, you know yourself
You don't know shit

You're a selfish, ignorant, rude ass little girl
You need a reality check because the world
don't revolve around you
You can go buy a pair of new shoes to suppress
your anger or pain for that matter
You can buy the latest outfit and hang with yo
girls like everything is ok but it's not
WHO GIVES A DAMN!

You can go all through your life, hunting for
Mr. Right when you kept running into Mr.
Wrong
Talking to this guy, talking to that guy, and get
this number and take that number down

FIRE

Once you learn them all, your dumb ass still
ain't happy
I told you that Mr. Right sat before you...***ME!***
And it's something that you're so blinded when
I am talking about you.

You ruined the one side of me that can never be
bought back
You ruined the day you walked in and lied to
me about loving me
Then you hold against me the one attachment to
me that means so much
Use this one soul against me and to think I am
suppose to be your friend
I hate you for everything you've done to me; I
hope that you are out of my life forever

You broke that wall, the wall that held my heart
It revealed something in me that I never thought
was there
I pity you, you, you and you if any of you cross
my path
Because when you all do, you all are in for a
rude awakening
I tried to be peaceful, peaceful wasn't good
enough you need someone to kick yo ass!

For any woman that toyed with my feelings and
I am not making exceptions
It's a woman that has hurt me one way or
another and you know exactly who you are
***WHEN YOU CROSS ME I ONLY GOT TWO
FINGERS FOR YOU!***

EMANCIPATION

THEN SEND YOUR ASS ON YOUR WAY
ROT BITCHES, ROT FOR EVERY DAMN
THING YOU EVER SAID TO ME OUT OF
THE WAY

EVERYTIME YOU BROKE MY HEART,
JUGGLING WITH MY FEELINGS
THAT GOES TO NOT JUST ONE BUT ALL
WOMEN THAT HAVE HURT ME!
I REFUSE TO TOLERATE IT
POOF! BE GONE, BECAUSE THE VERY
PERSON YOU THOUGHT I WAS OUT TO
BE, IS GONE!

FIRE

THINGS THAT I WANTED TO SAY TO MY EX (PART I)

You told me that I was good, but not good
enough.
So what is good to you?
I recall doing a million and one things to please
you but never good enough, it's okay.
I will move on and find someone that will
appreciate me
You're young and will never appreciate a good
man even if it's right there dead in your face.

Don't remember the last time any of your
current boyfriends after me aide you when you
needed help
Like to change your tire that caught flat and you
didn't know how to change it
Provide you a ride back and forth to work so
you wouldn't have to get on the bus to run late
in the rain, sleet, and snow
Or the early mornings, I would get out of bed
(when I didn't want to) come help you cause
you was stuck

Remember the times when I brought you to my
house to spend time and to get you away from
your issues
Just the thought of being together and how
much happiness we shared
Meant a lot to me of having you in my life, just
brighten up my entire world.

144

EMANCIPATION

In exchange for my very own life I would have
given you my last breath
Just to let you know how important you were to
me

But as before you let me down and I was the
fool for keeping you around
You've hurt me mentally, physically, verbally,
and emotionally
You allowed your friends, family, and whoever
to predict the ending of our relationship
You cared more for your exes than me; as you
did in our past
I was over mine and my whole entire focus was
all on you
And you wondered why you go through all the
stress you go through
Still haven't found the man that you want to
spend the rest of your life with.

You're still going through some things and
never can put the pieces of the puzzle together
You don't know how to treat people that were
always in your corner
Maybe I should have cheated and who knows if
I did, I will never tell you the truth
I was beneficial to you than any man you ever
been with but you said I wasn't good enough
I gave you more credit than any of my exes
because you were my completion to my life
You were like the air to my cold body, you gave
me life

FIRE

Questions if you really loved me and if you took
our relationship seriously
Just strangers, you would be someone I
wouldn't even think twice about now
You lost this affect on me
Your loss and it's another woman's gain in the
future

On a KAISERRIFIC note….

I'M DONE WITH YOU!!!!!
See if I ever come to your aide ever again
You can't call me your superman anymore
If you should ever fall on your back, don't look
around waiting for me to enter and pick you up
You can call whoever you been dealing with
I finished writing this chapter of my life, it's
done
You are a closed chapter in my life
You are one of the three contributions on my
feelings to relationships

Keep your calls, texts, or whatever to yourself...
I don't want to hear a thing you have to say
about this piece
I write from my heart and my soul
Your pain was the last you added to my hurt
I wished that I never fell in love with you!
I don't need your pitiful excuses, explanations,
lies and stories to this or to that
DON'T EVEN COMMENT ON MY SHIT,
BECAUSE YOUR WORDS DON'T MEAN A
DAMN THING TO ME!

EMANCIPATION

Your questionable thought of love is no existent
in my thoughts
You can leave out and don't let the door hit you
where the sun doesn't shine
I'm through with you......

*I thought expressing the way I felt would get
a lot off my chest. This also helps anyone that
has gone through anything similar. Love is a
very deep and passionate feeling. To spend
plenty of time into learning someone and
growing with someone would get you all torn up
and hurt. I valued this person very much
because I felt so much of a difference from what
I had encountered before. But when you meet
someone take your time and learn as much
about as you can.*

- *Kaiserrific*

(*Originally written in the summer of 2010*)

147

WIND UP DOLL

I was your wind up doll
That belonged to you for such a long time
Till some years ago you gave up on me
Gave up on what we could have had with each
other
I remember it like yesterday
One Wednesday night I never forget 8 years ago

Meeting through a mutual friend on the phone
We kicked it off real good
Learning everything that we can about each
other
Finding out things that no one else ever knew
Or at least I thought I did
Then it was time to meet
I came to your house and it kicked off a
relationship that will never be like any other one

The first time we had sex was so fire
I swore I fell in love with you
Exploring every part of our bodies
Doing things that I have never done with any
other woman
Made a whole new person out of me
Teaching things that I can do to you but also
worked well on other women

When I bring up the whole relationship idea
It was a good idea because we were so good for
one another

EMANCIPATION

But you said it wasn't right because we knew
how we were
We both look for love in all the wrong places
When we had love right here in our faces

I remember coming over to your house after
work
Those Friday nights were always my favorites
Cause we would lay there in your bed after sex
Lay together listening to the Quiet Storm until it
went off
I enjoy the moment of just me and you

Sex with you was not the norm
We explored each other as if we were in love
The freeze pops
Chocolate syrup
The ice cubes
You name it, we did it
The memories continue to play back in my head

But you wind me up only for your benefits
Less the thoughts of my feelings
Just knowing that if I resisted you from getting
close to me
'Cause I knew you was about to play with my
heart
Playing with the very thing that was closest to
me

Used sex as a way to win me over if I was
pissed at you
You knew how you do things to me

FIRE

Soaking me up in your wetness
Rusting up my heart to shutting me down
In the end, I was no good for the next woman

But there were times you played with my heart
Because you knew I was growing close to you
To make sure we didn't get closer,
You would distance yourself immediately
before I could say anything, you was gone
Because you wouldn't want to ruin a friendship
that we had
A close bond but ain't that too late now
You said, "I do"

I remember that one Thanksgiving evening we
shared in your truck
Was the first time I did anything in the open
public with you
But with you, it was always a new experience
for me
I could have gotten in trouble because I had my
responsibilities
And you had yours but that didn't matter
between us

I remember times you came by the apartment to
talk about love
And how it felt not to be getting it by the one
you love
I would hold you, one thing lead to another
We had sex again as always it was great
You cry afterwards because you felt like you
cheated,

EMANCIPATION

When you had no idea what he was doing

He used you for your truck
Only had sex with you either for convenience or
cause you begged him to
Then he would stare at the clock every now and
then to see how long it was going to last
But you loved him and said "I do" to him
Never looked back to me
You say because I was always there when you
needed a rescue
You was so phony
Walking around in your mask pretending to be
someone else
I knew who you were

See you put everyone else ahead of me
I was on your back burner
Your last option
When all else fails
I was the one your knew would be right there

Right there to provide comfort
Love like feelings
Intimate moments
Make you feel like a woman in every way I can
Wind up doll

You wound me up when needed to
Work me like a little robot when in the
beginning it wasn't like that
You made me feel like more than anything

FIRE

More than what anyone made me felt like in
years
But hey he got the prize of being in your public
eye
While you put me back on the shelf

But actually you took me to a thrift store and
gave me away
You was like, I don't need it anymore
Give it to a good home
Didn't even kiss me goodbye
Your wind up doll is gone

You've gone on with your life
Found someone to hold you at night
Where once I was there
A new man to share your laughs with
Where we would share those laughs

You went on to marry
Made your way to find happiness
Happiness that you and I once shared
But that's life,
Always someone better that comes along

But a wind up doll you made me out to be…

Outro

MY ESCAPE

(My Love and Appreciation)

Words Cannot Express My Appreciation

POETRY:
MY FRIEND, MY BITCH, MY LOVE

See I love you like I love my favorite song
You never left me and that's why we get along
I can keep reading you over and over until you
make some sense
And as always you don't make me feel any less
You are my therapy from my unleveled reality
A therapy that travels my mind from one
adventure to another
Allows me to make a new friend, some female's
lover, or to even hide undercover

I know when I want to be expressive you're
always there
With the words that I use, I can always make
you out to care
Pull out a pen and a piece of paper to begin
writing my craft
Sitting there in my favorite spot starting on the
first rough draft

I write for you
Express to you
React to your audience's responses
You make people aware of what's going on
You turn me on by the move of the pen
I will never leave you ever, ever again
To create beautiful pieces that can allow myself
to be who I am

MY ESCAPE

As a musician is a slave to the rhythm, I am a
slave of the melody made by the pen
I work for you
I strive for your excellence
To be an example of your beautiful words and
animated sayings
A new found creativity that continues to grow
and grow in people
But an old friend you always been to me
A true friend that has never left me
Poetry, you are my friend, my love, my
everything
A friend forever throughout my entire time of
living
Forever we are tied together

Poetry, you inspired so many including me
It's because of you, Poetry, that I had the
opportunity to meet some of the most intelligent
people that hit the stage
People that took the stage with courage
Reciting verses that reflects every personality of
a person in the audience
Vital information that grabbed my undivided
attention
Reassuring me that what they felt was very
important

Through poetry is the manner words come alive
The way one speaks, spits, acts or however you
want to interpret it
To articulate things that meant most to them
We are forever thankful to you poetry

FIRE

I love you poetry
And so does everyone else that lives by the
books too
It's a relationship that I don't have to worry
about leaving me
We will always have communication
A universal understanding between one another
A special connection that I can trust and know
will never breakup with me
And who would want to break up with poetry?

Don't be ashamed of what you know and love
about poetry!
How many of you cannot say that poetry has
changed your life?
How many of you can honestly say that you
learned a lot from poetry?
How many of you can say that poetry has never
made you understand anything?
How many times have you said that poetry has
not only told your story or told about a situation
in your life?

You would be a lie if you say that it hasn't
POETRY IS YOU!
POETRY IS ME!
Poetry is anyone that applies the pen to the
paper
To create a series filled with madness, sadness,
or pain
Or to write a piece of happiness, hope, and
inspiration with some self gain

MY ESCAPE

SNAP YOUR FINGERS HIGH!
Take these words to heart and carry it home as a
token
As these words of wisdom are spoken
Poetry, you are my friend, my love, my
everything
As beautiful as rivers flow peacefully into the
ocean
This masterpiece is a signature of my true
devotion

*Strongly inspired by my friends of the spoken
word community in St. Louis, MO again thank
you...*

157

About the Author

Kaiserrific is a St. Louis native and proud graduate from the Normandy School District. He is an accomplished thespian who portrayed several roles in such productions during his high school and college years. A close friend referred to him as the "Picasso of the pen and pad" which he carefully applies his deepest thoughts and feelings directly into his work. His inspiration evolves from his own personal observations as well the observation of people and their adaptation to life. One of his many great inspirations is his son Kemonee from whom he listens and learns. Kaiserrific is also a local spoken word artist; singer and dancer featured at varied St. Louis venues. Kaiserrific is very excited about the release of this debut book "FIRE" and soon will be completing his next upcoming book that will be released in the summer of 2012.

By Ronda Goolsby

THE CREATIVE TEAM OF FIRE

Kaiserrific
Author/Co-Creative Consultant over Book Layout & Cover Design/Co-Editor
www.kaiserrific.webs.com

MEET THE TEAM BEHIND FIRE

THE MOST TALENTED PEOPLE THAT PUT HARD WORK AND DEDICATION INTO THIS BOOK.

C. Lynne Luster
Advisor/Creative Consultant/Editor
www.team-c3.com

Cynthia Jowers
(*A.k.a. X Blu Rayne Poet*)
Advisor/Co-Editor of Book Layout
www.xblurayne.com

Jason Humphreys
Graphic Designer of the Book Cover
www.fairviewphotography.com

Kathleen Humphreys
(*Fairview Photography*)
Creative Consultant/Photography
www.fairviewphotography.com

Mea M. Hampton
(*New Generation VA Solutions*)
Advisor/Co-Editor/Creative Consultant/Editor of Book Layout
www.newgenerationva.com

Poet Janet Dawson
Advisor/Creative Consultant
www.janetdawson.webs.com

Made in the USA
Charleston, SC
23 February 2012